THE TREK

Adventure and Enlightenment
on a Climb to the Summit of
Kala Patthar, Above Mount Everest
Base Camp in the Himalayas

DAVID SCHACHNE

D1247250

For all of my girls

Contents

Acknowledgements

T his book could not have been written without the love and support of my family. For many years, I have been an absentee dad and husband, first due to my job and travel schedule and then due to working on my manuscript day and night while locked in the "dungeon." To the four ladies in my life, thank you for putting up with me. Faith, you are my "Wonder Woman" in every way. You're an incredible wife, and you absolutely belong in the "Mother's Hall of Fame." You are selfless. Our children are lucky to have a mom like you – and there's no question I hit the jackpot marrying you. Tori, bring harmony to the world. You have been given the tools. Lexie, reach for the stars, in so many different ways. Reece, the way to (most) people's heart is through their stomach. Pursue your passion.

Sherry Suib Cohen, thank you, thank you, thank you. I never thought my manuscript had any potential until we met. Your feedback was the pure inspiration I needed to "stick with it" after years of thinking this was always going to be a pet project. I carried your "words of encouragement" in my pocket for a very long time and I read them anytime I went off course. You challenged me like no other. You are truly an incredible woman. Jennifer Goldstein, all I can say is "like mother, like daughter." Your insight took my journey into unchartered territory. I thank you dearly for this. And Bruce Douglas, Heath Grayson, Jennifer Josephy, Jeff Oestreicher, Matt Oestreicher, and of course, my four girls, thank you all for your input and guidance.

Last but not least, mom and dad, thanks for bringing me into this world and raising me in a way that enabled me to have the passion I do for so many different things. Mom, I've always been amazed at how you pulled off raising four kids while dad was never home. You should be proud. Dad, thanks for instilling a strong work ethic in me and teaching me about generosity.

Preface

T his is a story of a guy who dreamed big, but thought little, of what was in store for him on a trek in the Himalayas. It is my story, and it is based on a daily travel journal that I kept for almost three weeks in the autumn of 2004, during a trek to the summit of Kala Patthar in Nepal, nearly 18,200 feet above sea level. Kala Patthar is approximately 700 feet higher than Mount Everest Base Camp and offers one of the most spectacular, close-up views of Mount Everest. The summit of Everest cannot be seen from Everest Base Camp.

When I returned home, I added specific details to each of the daily diary entries. I also added some material to the story based on research, as well as some past experiences during my life. All of these experiences, from the trek and from my past, happened to me as I recorded them here. To protect the privacy of others, I have changed most names.

I have reproduced excerpts, specifically; daily agendas, menus and descriptions, verbatim, from the brochure that the travel company provided to us. This information is listed at the start of each new day. I have also taken the liberty of providing a "more accurate" version of what the travel company *should* have actually said in the brochure. This information is listed in *italics* at the end of each day.

To be very clear, this is not a story of a daring climbing expedition to the summit of Mount Everest or K2 or any of the dozens of fabulously high peaks in the Himalayas. There are hundreds of those stories, generally describing in great detail the travails, triumphs and frequent failures of world-class mountaineers, and the dangers they endured during their journeys. Tragically, many of those books are written not by the climbers who reached those summits, or attempted to reach them, but instead by their friends, companions, spouses, or others who are telling the story of their friends or loved ones who didn't make it back home alive.

My story is vastly different. It is not one of an elite climber. Rather, it is of an average Joe (or in this case, Dave), who was by no means a hard-core athlete. I was, at the time of this trek, just an ordinary family man, in good, but certainly not great, physical shape, with an office job and a gym membership. To stay in shape, I worked out on the treadmill or the stair master, and once every couple of years or so, would take a weekend hiking trip with some friends. Many of those trips were to climb tall peaks throughout the United States. They were difficult climbs, and definitely challenging, but still manageable. In my youth, I had been in excellent physical shape, but like so many other middle-aged men, I ultimately spent too much time at the office, became lazy (and tired) and put on a few extra pounds.

The only noteworthy factor that set me apart from most of my peers was that I had dreamed, for years, of visiting a place that, in my mind, loomed as the most magnificent destination in the world – the Himalayas.

Born and raised in Brooklyn, New York, I hadn't experienced much of the natural world prior to turning twelve years old. I grew up in a brick row house, one of forty or so in a line nearly the length of three football fields. The public park down the street from my home was constructed almost entirely of concrete, so that nothing in the park would be destroyed or stolen. There wasn't a single blade of grass growing in it. My house had a twelve-foot by twelve-foot garden in front, with a round, three-foot wide, man-made pond around which my parents placed a flock of plastic, pink flamingos. As a little kid, I thought it was so cool that mine was the only house on the block with a mini-oasis in his front yard.

The back of my house was an alleyway, used as a parking lot. While the dads were at work during the day, it became a play area for the neighborhood kids. My favorite pastime in the alleyway was playing basketball with a tiny, pink Spalding (Spaldeen) Hi-bounce ball, purchased for twenty-nine cents. The basketball hoop was a four-inch opening that existed between the brick façade of my house and the utility wiring above my garage.

My elementary school and middle school also lacked grass fields, so for sports, I played stickball, stoopball, punch ball, paddleball and street hockey (on quad roller skates) – all sports played against concrete walls, on paved sidewalks, or asphalt roads. If I wasn't playing one of these urban sports, my friends and I would take over the roads in front of our houses and play one of many classic street games such as spud, skully, ringoleavio or red-rover. We constantly risked being run over by cars speeding down the street. In the evenings, our favorite past time was stepping on giant water bugs that swarmed out of the sewers on hot summer days. I think we recorded over 1,000 dead bodies one evening, before we finally gave up counting. Fond memories.

The summer before I turned thirteen, I was fortunate to be able to attend sleep-away camp in the Catskill Mountains in upstate New York, where I fell in love with nature and the great outdoors. For the first time in my life, I hiked, camped outdoors, water-skied, and went canoeing down the Delaware River. It opened my eyes to the natural beauty the world had to offer. I spent the next four summers going back to Camp Beaver Lake in Monticello, New York, and then went cross-country the following summer, camping out in dozens of national parks.

Not only were those summers the most memorable of my life, they were also the best days of my childhood. And even now, any natural setting – it doesn't matter what kind – brings out the best in me and reminds me of those wonderful times. The more unique the setting, such as the Grand Canyon, Yosemite, or Joshua Tree National Park, the more enraptured I become. These truly spectacular places, whether mountains, rivers, rock formations, waterfalls, or forests, bring me utter joy.

Prior to this trek, hiking in the Himalayas had been something I had desperately wanted to do for more than two decades. Of course, there were other destinations I wanted to see – places on my personal "bucket list" – but none like the Himalayas. As to why (besides the natural beauty of it), I really had no idea at the time. I only knew my life had felt unfulfilled. For years, even though I had a decent job and a wonderful and loving family, I felt something was missing. There was a hole I needed to fill, somehow. I had no idea what it was, but it bothered me constantly and I needed to try to figure it out.

I had thus hoped that this trek would provide some answers, or at a minimum, some sense of satisfaction. So, when I turned forty in 2001, I booked the trek as a birthday present to myself. Then, one month prior to my departure, the September 11th attacks occurred. I didn't want to leave my family at such a terrible time, so I regretfully cancelled my plans and forfeited my payment.

A few years passed and the burning passion grew more overwhelming. Finally, in late 2004, I was able to arrange the time off from work and received the go-ahead from my wife Faith. (It was important to me that she was okay with it, since I was going to be gone for more than three weeks; it was an expensive trip; and most important, there were many risks.) So, I plunked down $3,000 and with some apprehension, signed the waivers that indemnified the trekking company against any loss of life or limb. They were well aware of the dangers and didn't want a lawsuit if by some chance I got hurt...or worse.

I knew, based on the significant research I had done, that people who trek in the Himalayas inevitably get sick – from all sorts of things, but mostly gastrointestinal disease. I also knew the weather would be cold, but according to my research and based on the time of year I would be trekking, not unusually so. I believed I could, and would, work through any potential problems – whether stomach issues, altitude sickness, cold weather, or anything else. I had previously reached the high summits of plenty of mountains around the world, although not nearly as high as 18,000 feet. Each and every time, I dealt with all sorts of unexpected challenges along the way, but managed just fine. And I've faced other types of physical adversity, such as hiking twenty-six miles for eight hours through the hot desert for the Annual Bataan Memorial Death March at the White Sands

Missile Range in New Mexico. There, I marched in ninety-five degree heat, forging through thick, heavy sand, with the sun searing my skin for hours, and blisters eating away at my feet until they were bloody. I knew the pain I experienced was nothing compared to what our captured servicemen had endured on their eighty-mile march during World War II in the Philippines, so I continued on in order to honor them.

In each and every one of my previous experiences with physically demanding adventures, I persevered because I knew the fear, the discomfort, the pain, and the exhaustion, were always temporary. So I would just grin and bear it, knowing it would all soon come to an end. This trek was different…more than I could have ever imagined.

Are you ready to take a hike?

PREFACE

1

ANXIETY

"What we anticipate seldom occurs, what we least expected generally happens."

-Benjamin Disraeli

TRAVEL BROCHURE:

Day 1-3: NEW YORK TO KATHMANDU • 4,383 feet

Travel from your home port to Kathmandu. All flights departing the US cross the dateline and consequently a day is lost. Arrive in Kathmandu, where a guide will meet you. Check into a classic four-star hotel located in the popular Thamel district. Great food from all over the world, fabulous shopping, and Durbar square with its numerous temples and markets are nearby. While we wrap up last minute paperwork with the Nepali government, you will have a casual day for shopping, visiting the palaces, Durbar Square, Hindu temples and shrines, Buddhist stupas, or just relaxing at the hotel. A favorite destination is the Monkey Temple, a Buddhist temple situated on a small hill that offers panoramic views of the city. Or you can join the thousands of Hindus who venture to the Pashupatinath temple, one of the most famous Hindu temples in Nepal and the most famous Shiva temple in Asia.

My first entry into my journal, on the flight to Tokyo

It's been a few hours since I said goodbye to Faith and my daughters – Tori, Lexie and Reece, ages 11, 10 and 6 respectively. As we were parting, Faith handed me a typically thoughtful gift, this travel journal. The start of this long flight, the first of several, seems like the right time to begin writing. As I opened it for the very first time, I saw this loving note from Faith written on the first page.

11/5/04

Dear David,

I can't believe it - your departure date is finally here. You have waited a long time for this, and I am so excited for you. There aren't many people who have a dream and actually make it happen. You are a great role model for our children. I hope that this will teach them to try to live out their dreams and reach for the stars too! While you are away, please enjoy yourself to the fullest, be careful, take good care of yourself and do not worry about us at home. We will be fine. I will not spend a lot of time on the phone and I will take great care of our girls. I love you very much and will be thinking of you every day and every night. Enjoy yourself and know that I will always love you.

Faith

CHAPTER ONE: ANXIETY

My first thought is I must be crazy for flying to the Himalayas, attempting to climb to 18,200 feet above sea level. Seriously, what on earth am I doing? I know in all likelihood it will work out fine and I will see my family in a few weeks, but there's still this small sliver of doubt – a fatalistic feeling I have whenever I travel, because of September 11th.

I flew out to California on a business trip from New York on September 10th, 2001, about a dozen hours before that tragic event. I arrived in the late evening, checked in to my hotel, and went straight to bed. The next morning, I woke up and turned on the television and saw the replay of the first plane hitting the North Tower. You know the rest. Long story short, I ended up driving back to New York from California with a business associate. The long drive gave me plenty of time to think about how it could have been me on one of those planes if I had flown the next morning. I had flown extensively for business, approximately one million miles, in the eleven years prior to September 11th. In the three years following September 11th, prior to going on this trek, I hardly flew at all.

I knew it was going to be difficult to say goodbye to my girls. Driving to the airport, Faith and I made small talk to avoid discussing the possible dangers. Tori and Lexie were clearly concerned, but they didn't say anything. Reece didn't understand the fears we were all experiencing, so she was her typical carefree self. Her innocence was comforting. Faith tried to crack her usual bad jokes, which made Tori roll her eyes, as always.

At the drop-off area at the airport, I gave the girls lots of hugs and kisses. When Faith and I said goodbye, we didn't have too much to say to each other. We had discussed everything ad nauseam in preparation for my departure – the trip, the kids, what to do in case of an emergency, etc. So we just hugged for a while, looked at each other, kissed, hugged again, and then as she stepped into the car, she gave me the journal and told me to record the entire trek. Then I watched her drive away.

Faith and I almost never exchange gifts, no matter what the occasion. We've always believed we have all of the basic necessities in life, so it's unnecessary to shower each other with needless things. Yet, she will surprise me sometimes with just the right thing.

Evening, on the flight to Tokyo

There are five more hours to go on my flight from New York to Tokyo. I haven't slept at all. I'm anxious and over-tired. The past few nights at home have been relatively sleepless ones spent thinking about all of the "what-ifs." What if our antiquated airplane breaks down or crashes while flying into the Himalayas? What if I get hurt on the trek at 18,000 feet? What if I have an asthma attack on the summit of Kala Patthar? The list of concerns swirled around my brain constantly

This trek is something I feel I was compelled, or destined, to do. I love to hike and I relish being in the mountains. However, I don't know if this love of hiking is strong enough to outweigh the risks. And to top it all off, I'm very sick with a terrible head and chest cold and a dreadful, hacking cough from bronchitis. As a result, my asthma is acting up as well. I have had this same type of cold around this time of year, for the past six years, and it persists for a few months at a time and it always transitions from a cold into bronchitis. I should have paid more attention to this as a potential source of trouble.

By some crazy coincidence, the woman sitting next to me on this flight is going to the Himalayas as well. Her name is Donna and she is very sweet and attractive – slim, nearly six feet tall, with blue eyes and dirty blond hair. She is going to attempt to climb Ama Dablam. At over 22,000 feet, Ama Dablam is one of the most impressive and beautiful mountains in the world.

Donna checked her bags all the way through to Nepal. I should have done the same. I hadn't wanted to take a chance that my gear would get lost in transit, so I decided not to check it. Now I'm going to be lugging my massive army duffel from flight to flight to flight to flight – four flights in total.

11-8-04
(Crossed over the International Date Line into Tokyo)
Evening

It's Monday evening and I'm still in Tokyo. I arrived at 3:30 P.M. after flying for thirteen hours. I've been sitting in the airport departure area for four hours waiting for my second flight to Bangkok. Oddly, there were hardly any people around, except for Donna, for much of the time I've been here.

My next flight is already delayed an hour. With any luck, I will arrive in Thailand at 1:00 A.M. and will hang out at the airport. The airport terminal here has the same boring stores as most airports I've travelled through. It's great that I have this journal to write in to occupy some time, since I already finished reading through the dozens of magazines and newspapers I brought with me.

I had gyoza dumplings for dinner. Eating them reminded me of the trip Faith and I took to Japan thirteen years ago as newlyweds. We found a real dive with delicious dumplings for a bargain price and we ended up eating dumplings for three straight days for breakfast, lunch, and dinner. We wisely didn't ask what was actually inside them. We were young, foolish, in love and poor. We couldn't afford much else in Japan.

The dumplings tasted as good today as they did back then, with their soy sauce sodium kick. I have to admit, I am a dumpling fiend. I buy them frozen at the supermarket, I always order them at Chinese restaurants, and I even order them for dinner at classic American establishments like The Cheesecake Factory, where they are called "pot stickers." Of course, I order them fried whenever possible. It's the only way to really enjoy dumplings – at their most unhealthy and fattening pan-fried state. Fortunately, I don't have to worry about gaining weight on this trip. I need carbs, carbs, and more carbs to power myself up the mountain each day.

I'm rambling. I am in serious need of some sleep.

THE TREK

11-9-04
Mid-morning

When I arrived at the airport in Thailand at 1 A.M. this morning, it was stifling hot in the terminal due to a lack of air-conditioning. There was a nine-hour layover until my next flight to Kathmandu. So I decided to go across the road to a hotel to get a few hours of sleep, where I was given a pleasantly modern and clean room. However, I still didn't get much sleep. Those anxious thoughts continued to circle in my brain and I was terribly over-tired. I tried blocking out my thoughts, and even tried counting sheep. Nothing worked.

I ran into Donna at the airport this morning and had a long breakfast with her — believe it or not, dumplings. We talked about many different subjects including life, jobs, hiking, and climbing. She told me she has climbed mountains all over the world. After this trip, she wants to take a break from work and have a child. She informed me she has one slight problem. She doesn't have a husband or a boyfriend. I wasn't really sure why she was telling me this, considering we had just met yesterday. Just the same, I immediately thought to myself "Wow, I could probably help her out." ("Why else would she have told me?" my male ego asked.) Luckily, I quickly realized this was a case of temporary insanity on my part caused by my lack of sleep. I was delusional for even thinking she would extend me an invitation and even more so for entertaining the thought of being unfaithful.

It's an amazingly wild coincidence that she will be staying at the exact same hotel in Kathmandu where I am staying. It's bizarre to get on a plane in New York City and sit next to a beautiful woman who is travelling half way around the world, on four different flights, and find out she is staying at the same hotel on the opposite side of the planet. She didn't even book her climb with the same trekking company I did. What are the odds of something like this happening? Some people would call this

15

happenstance, but I call it fate. Maybe something is, in fact, supposed to happen between us. Maybe there is a reason we met. Or then again, maybe God is testing me. If so, it's surely tempting. Fortunately, I'm a superstitious guy. If I misbehave, I have no doubt I'll pay for it dearly on the mountain. I'm probably already in trouble, just for having the slightest thought about being unfaithful, especially to someone named Faith.

I firmly believe every person you meet in life you meet for a reason or a purpose. It's up to each one of us to then take the appropriate next steps, if any, that will ignite a chain of events potentially impacting one's life forever. I've thought about this so many times in the past, mainly for one reason. Something happened to me years ago that I'll never forget.

I had recently graduated from college and I was in Frankfurt, Germany for a few months, to work as an apprentice in a feather and down factory that manufactured pillows. While there, I spent most of my weekends travelling. One day, I was in the central rail station of some large European city (I can't recall which one.) While waiting in line to buy a ticket, I noticed that Meg Ryan, the actress, was standing right behind me. I recognized her from the soap opera "As the World Turns," which my mom watched almost every day when I was a teenager. Meg looked beautiful. I had had a teen crush since I first laid eyes on her on television. I so desperately wanted to strike up a conversation with her, but I didn't have the guts to do so. It was like a scene out of a comedy movie, where the geeky nerd is too shy to make his move and he misses out on his one and only chance in life to hook up with the hottest girl in school. Who knows where fate would have taken us or what chain of events this one move would have set off. Okay, I know…I'm now having delusions of grandeur. Besides, if I had in fact dated Meg Ryan (as far-fetched as that may sound), I may not have met Faith and had our three wonderful daughters. It's frightening to contemplate how easily our destinies can be derailed. Regardless, ever since that geek moment, I've always told myself, and eventually my kids as well, that if you don't try to grab the brass ring, you'll never get it.

Afternoon

We finally arrived into Kathmandu, Nepal at 12:30 P.M. – thirty-six long and mostly sleepless hours after taking off from New York. I'm in my hotel room and my head is in a complete fog, but I need to attempt to stay awake until tonight. I have serious jetlag, but if I don't adjust my body clock to the time difference here as fast as possible, I'll be doomed on the trek. Nepal is almost nine hours ahead of New York time, so my body needs to adjust and adapt to virtually the complete opposite time zone from home.

Upon arriving, I joined up with some of the trekking group members who had already convened at the airport and we took a bus to the hotel. The bus was old, rickety, hot, and malodorous. The smell, my exhaustion, and too many dumplings over the past 48 hours were making me seriously nauseated, so I concentrated on looking out the filthy window.

As we drove through Nepal's capital, with its' one million inhabitants making it by far its largest city, the extreme poverty was obvious. Sitting at a relatively modest altitude of 4,600 feet, Kathmandu is more than 2,000 years old and is showing its age.

Large crowds of people throng the broken pavements in ragged garb. There is utter filth and litter everywhere. Residential buildings are made from bare gray concrete, with only hollow squares where you would normally see windows. Instead, wet blankets and clothes hang in the empty spaces, drying in the hot air.

Many of the buildings appear to be heavily damaged and in desperate need of repair. Almost all the facades and roofs have massive cracks. From earthquakes? I wondered uneasily. If these buildings were in New York City, or anywhere else in the U.S., they'd be condemned and demolished.

The hotel we are staying at is in the middle of the city. I wasn't sure what to expect, since I had not checked it out on the web prior to my departure. After seeing so much of Kathmandu on the bus ride to the hotel, I lowered my expectations a notch.

Upon arrival however, we were confronted with a grand, palatial building smack in the midst of all the poverty. There was a large gate at the front of the entrance with a security guard. We drove into the circular driveway and saw the lush gardens in the back of the property. I was impressed.

Looks can be deceiving. My room is not much bigger than a walk-in closet. The carpet is completely worn and has multiple reddish black stains in it – possibly blood. The room is dirty, dusty, and has a strong odor of mildew. The hotel has a four-star rating and is considered upscale in Nepal, but is basically inferior to any low-priced budget motel in the U.S. The mattress is shabby, but luckily has a board underneath for support.

I discovered the air conditioner wasn't working, so I called the front desk to have them send up someone to fix it. I waited impatiently in the stuffy, sweltering room. Opening the windows didn't help at all. I spent some time organizing my bags to get ready for the trek and then rested on the bed, closing my eyes, anxiously pondering what the next two weeks had in store for me. I fought hard to not fall asleep.

While waiting, I thought of how I've always had crazy things happen to me on hiking trips. I immediately recalled the time Faith and I went to Joshua Tree National Park in California. Our daughter Tori was less than a year old at the time, so we didn't want to travel without her.

It was late evening by the time we arrived at the park. We checked into a place that informed us that they didn't have any rooms in the main building, but instead would be "upgrading" us and putting us up in one of their secluded cabins, a mile or so down a long, dirt road. We drove there in total darkness, except for the car headlights which were lighting up the path and revealing the hundreds of moths being attracted to the beams. After a couple of minutes, we arrived at the isolated cabin. Most people would have considered it romantic, being so secluded without another human being in sight. However, we had Tori with us, and Faith and I both had a similarly eerie feeling. Faith asked me if I thought it was safe and I assured her it would be okay. Of course, I had no idea and knew I could be mistaken. We opened the door to the small, four hundred square foot cabin, and entered. There was only one main room with a double bed. There was no telephone in the room and we didn't own a cell phone yet. We set a couple of blankets on the floor and placed Tori on top of them, warmly wrapped. Faith suggested leaving the lights on in the room, since she was a bit nervous. I wasn't going to argue with her, especially since I was a bit freaked out myself. We all fell asleep.

At approximately two o'clock in the morning, in a deep sleep, I heard a loud banging. Initially, I thought I was dreaming. The banging continued, and eventually, Faith screamed out to me "David, there is someone staring at us." Wide awake now, I turned my head and saw a middle-aged man, his face worn and unshaven, staring through the window at Faith and I in our bed, with Tori very visibly exposed lying on the floor. The man saw us both of us, clearly freaked out and frightened. We look right into his bulging eyes and he yelled to us through the window "My car broke down a half mile up the road and I need money for gas. Can you help me out?" In that split second, my heart immediately started pounding out of my chest, beating exponentially faster than it had just a few seconds earlier when I had first laid eyes on the man. I felt the blood rush through my body toward my muscles, in order to better prepare them for the strength and speed I might need. Whenever I heard someone ask for money for gas in the past, I knew it was just an excuse to get a few dollars from me. Besides, we were a mile off the main road.

I shouted out the first thing that came to mind. "I'm sorry, but I don't have any money! Please leave." The man, looking very disappointed, disappeared from view. Faith and I looked at each other and she said. "David, we can't stay here. What if he comes back knowing we're helpless? What if he is here with other people? What if he has a gun? We don't have a phone. We need to get help."

We jumped out of bed and packed up our things in about three minutes flat. I reached into one of the pockets and grabbed my Swiss army knife and pulled out the largest blade. I told Faith I was going to go outside and make sure there was nobody there. I also told her to lock the door behind me as soon as I went out and to not open it until I came back. And I told her if I didn't return in two minutes, to start screaming for help at the top of her lungs.

I looked out the window, using a flashlight to try to see the doorway and make sure the man wasn't standing near it. As far as I could tell, it looked clear. I told Faith I loved her. I opened the door, went outside and heard Faith bolt the door shut immediately behind me. I looked around the cabin, circling it fully, and then looked all around my car. No sign of the intruder. I started the car and pulled it right to the doorway of the cabin and ran inside, grabbed Tori and then our luggage, and jumped in the car with Faith and took off. We drove into the center of town in Twenty Nine Palms, California and checked into a place with a parking lot full of cars. I was never so happy to be staying in a Howard Johnson's motel.

I came back to my senses in Kathmandu after hearing a knock on my hotel door. The maintenance man arrived to fix the air conditioner, an hour after I called. After tinkering with it for a few minutes, he pressed the power button and immediately, a giant gray, dense cloud of dust blew into the room from the unit. It was the perfect trigger for my asthma. My lungs reacted immediately, resulting in a ten minute coughing marathon. I could barely see inside the room with the thick cloud of dust particles blowing into my eyes, up my nose, and all around me. When I called the front desk, I was told there were no other rooms available.

I decided to let the dust settle, so I went for a short walk by myself. However, a few blocks from the hotel, a large, black, malnourished cow decided to join me on my stroll. I could see its bones under its thin hide.

Cows are protected, sacred animals in Hinduism. It is taboo to kill cows or eat their meat because they are a symbol of life.

Oddly, however, they are also frequently neglected – except for once every year when they are celebrated, washed, and adorned for the Cow Holiday, or Gopastami as it is called. It was sad seeing the cow completely ignored by the crowds of pedestrians flowing through the streets, and it was so amazing that it knew to walk along the sidewalk with everyone else, instead of walking into the oncoming traffic. It even waited at a traffic light with me. Freaky.

The city, bustling with heavy traffic, was highly polluted, just like Bangkok, which I visited years ago with Faith after visiting Japan. The smog was so thick you could see the dense gray air all around you. It's no surprise my asthma is getting worse minute-by-minute. I only brought two inhalers with me on this trip and one of them is almost empty. I'll probably finish them both prior to reaching the summit of Kala Patthar. If I do, I'm in serious trouble.

I was approached by a couple of locals looking to exchange Nepalese rupees into dollars. I kept walking, just shaking my head and not even looking at them. I had had no interest in such transactions ever since Faith and I were ripped off in Warsaw ten years earlier. We had been traveling through Eastern Europe in the early 90's. I thought I'd be smart and try to make a few extra dollars by changing money on the black market. A middle-aged, questionable-looking character in a black leather jacket approached us. I asked him the exchange rate and it was easily ten percent more than I could get at the local bank, so I figured it was a no-brainer. I told him I'd like to change fifty dollars. He turned around, with his back to me, and counted the money. He then hands it to me and I hand him a $50 bill. He asked me to count it in front of him, which I did, and noticed he had shortchanged me two Polish zloty. He acted surprised and asked for it back, counting the money right in front of my eyes. When he finished counting, he agreed with my math, and pulled out the extra two zloty and added it to the batch of currency. I thanked him and he walked away. A few seconds later, having a suspicious feeling, I decided to count it again. Sure enough, he had somehow managed to remove a couple of the larger bills in the process of adding back the smaller bills. He obviously did this with the sleight of hand of a very talented magician. I hadn't noticed a thing. Of course, the guy disappeared into a store and exited the back door, never to be seen again. Faith and I agreed at that moment to never change money on the black market again.

After my walk, there was a get together with everyone on the trek. There are two men, George and Randy, from New Jersey; three men, Jack, Teddy and Mitch, from South Carolina; Jay, from Illinois; John, from Florida; Fernando, from Spain; Ian, from Ireland; two women, Robin, from Idaho, and Kim, from New Mexico; and a married couple, Bruce and Dakotah – the assistant guide – from Oregon. Lorraine, our guide and the leader of the trek, is from Utah. Both Lorraine and Dakotah, the two guides, are sturdy, attractive blondes, the strong outdoorsy types one would expect to find in this setting.

Evening

We went out for a group dinner tonight. Although we ordered a massive amount of food, it cost us just seven dollars each. I figured now was the time to get a taste of the local cuisine and ordered the Tibetan meal. Big mistake. Before I could even finish eating, my stomach started feeling queasy. Within seconds, I had to run to the bathroom like a horse out of the starting gate. When I opened the door, I wasn't prepared for what I saw, or rather, what I didn't see. Instead of a toilet, there was only a hole in the floor! With all of the travelling I have done internationally, I had completely forgotten that most third-world countries lack these modern-day bathroom fixtures and accompanying seats to which we in the West have become so accustomed.

Urgent, urgent, urgent! A loud siren was going off in my head. My insides were about to burst. My brain had to process this immediately. Luckily, based on the emergency, it was working in hyper-speed mode. I ripped my pants down, found my rightful place and then exploded with a blast greater than a neutron bomb. As I was crouching in place and enjoying the momentary satisfaction of having just relieved myself, a horrible, foreboding thought overwhelmed me. "This is probably the nicest bathroom I'll be seeing for almost three weeks."

As far back as I can recall, my stomach has always been extremely sensitive to nerves, foreign foods and certainly foreign organisms. Unfortunately, I am going to be dealing with all three of these factors simultaneously. It hit me that the next two weeks were going to be a complete disaster for my internal organs. My health was already starting to spiral out of control -- no sleep, awful asthma, a bad cold, a hacking cough -- and now I had to worry about a terrible stomach.

Some people in the group were smart enough to order Italian food, like pizza and pasta, which looked as good as any pizza I've eaten in the States. Lesson learned, "When in Nepal, do what the Romans do."

The only good news from this evening is that the people on my trek are all friendly. Unfortunately, most of them are traveling with at least one other person. Therefore, it may be a bit difficult to build a strong bond with any of them. The guys from South Carolina are the most outgoing – happy-go-lucky Southerners. Mitch, looking the most senior of the group with some graying hair, and Teddy, a stocky yet fit, middle-aged guy, are good friends. I would guess they are in their early 50's. Jack, much younger, is an acquaintance of theirs.

George, short, middle-aged, with a mustache, and always wearing a baseball cap, seems very nice. He is the kind of person who always has some connection to any conversation, no matter what the subject, and can seemingly click with anyone in a heartbeat. Randy, a friend of George's from home, was the complete opposite. Standing about six-foot three and also wearing a baseball cap, he didn't say a word at all the entire evening. Despite being opposites, or maybe because of it, they are apparently good friends.

The rest of the group, including the two single women, Robin and Kim, chimed in from time-to-time. Dakotah and her husband sat by and quietly observed the chatter. I think they were letting the group dynamic just take its course and seeing where it went.

Most of the discussions centered in on questions about the trip and what we should be expecting. Lorraine did a great job of providing as much detail as possible, as she did prior to our departure, a month or so ago. She called each of us in advance of the trek to get to know us a bit and to make sure we were all exercising hard, organizing our gear, and getting immunized.

11-10-04
Afternoon

I slept for only six hours last night, not nearly enough to fully catch up, but better than nothing. It's now late in the afternoon and my body is saying, "Get into the freaking bed and go to sleep," but I'm trying to avoid doing that. I tried to call Faith with my MCI telecom card. The operator at the hotel claimed to have never heard of MCI. So I tried ATT. When that didn't work either, I called Faith by direct dial and we talked for ten minutes, which would show up on my hotel bill as a fifty-dollar charge. Ouch.

I went on a tour of the city this morning with the rest of the group, even though I didn't feel well, since I figured I would not be back in Nepal for a very long time, if ever. We visited the Pashupatinath Temple, the largest Hindu temple of Lord Shiva in the world and apparently regarded as one of the most sacred. It was established in the fifth century and is the oldest Hindu temple in Kathmandu. Mughal invaders destroyed a significant part of the temple in the fourteenth century and little or nothing remains of the original fifth century temple exterior. The temple as it stands today was built in the nineteenth century. Believers in Pashupatinath, mainly Hindus, are allowed to enter the temple premises, but non-Hindu visitors are only allowed to view the temple from the across the bank of the Bagmati river. This worked fine for me. I wasn't really in a "sight-seeing" mood. There were monkeys everywhere, freely roaming the viewing area scouring for food, and whizzing and swinging by me, within inches of my face. At first, it was cute – for about a minute. Then it got really creepy.

Afterward, we went to another temple, the Boudhanath Stupa. It is one of the holiest Buddhist sites in Nepal and also one of the most popular tourist destinations in the Kathmandu area. It has been a place of rest and prayer for Tibetan merchants travelling to Kathmandu for centuries.

A stupa, whether small or massively large, as in this case, is a pile of earth or other material marking a holy site in honor of Buddha. The base of the stupa is surrounded with a brick wall with 147 niches, each with four or five prayer wheels which spin, engraved with the mantra, "om mani padme hum." The literal translation partially means 'jewel" and "lotus flower," but when combined, it has many different interpretations. The six syllables are supposed to represent the six realms of existence – generosity, ethics, patience, diligence, renunciation and wisdom. According to local belief, spinning the wheels amplifies the effect of chanting the mantra and it is basically good luck to spin them. So I spun them and spun them and chanted as much as I could. I figured I needed all the luck I could get in the next couple of weeks. Lorraine had to drag me away.

After the tour, I relaxed a while and then went out for a pizza with Jay and George. The pizza was surprisingly good. I decided at that moment that whenever I had the opportunity to order pizza, I would. If you think about it, it's tough to mess up a pizza – or get sick from eating it. There's just bread, sauce, and cheese. And if there are any devilish organisms living within or on top of any of those ingredients, they'll most certainly be destroyed in the extremely high heat of the oven.

Late evening

We went for a traditional Nepalese dinner earlier this evening – which turned out to be a very unpleasant experience in a total tourist trap. We waited almost two hours before we were able to eat. There was a Nepalese dance exhibition first, which went on for over an hour. We were all tired and anxious to begin our journey, but were forced to sit through it. We then finally had dinner and the only thing I ate was rice. Everything else brought to the table made my stomach turn.

Unfortunately, the "stomach bug" had already permeated my internal organs. Even only eating rice, which typically is binding, I had an absolutely awful stomachache immediately after dinner.

While crouching down and doing my thing in the bathroom, I noticed a couple of cockroaches, but I was feeling so bad that it didn't even faze me, even though I detest bugs, particularly roaches.

I recalled a crazy evening on my honeymoon, in 1990. Faith and I had flown into Hilo, on the Big Island of Hawaii, arriving in the early afternoon. We rented a car and drove to Kona on the opposite side of the Island, which took us a couple of hours. All was good. We checked into our hotel, did the typical stuff you do as newlyweds, and then headed out for dinner to a restaurant a few miles away from the hotel. After dinner, around 10 P.M., we returned to the car and I opened the passenger door for Faith. (Chivalry wasn't dead yet in our brand new marriage.) She was about to get into the car when she screamed at the top of her lungs. I couldn't understand what was wrong until I took a look in the car. The seats were swarming with hundreds of cockroaches. There was an infestation under one of the seats and once the day had turned into night, they came out from hiding. It was the most disgusting thing I had ever seen, up until this trek. We called the car rental company and they told us they would replace the car in the morning, but we needed to bring it to them. If that wasn't bad enough, while we were trying to kill the cockroaches for a good hour or two, we were being attacked by huge, pre-historic flying cockroaches as well (known as B-52's in Hawaii.) I figured the roaches in the car had called in the B-52's for reinforcement. They were flying directly into our heads like Kamikaze pilots.

When I returned to the table, Lorraine informed me she was getting concerned about my stomach issues and told me to start my dosage of ciprofloxacin, otherwise known as Cipro, a very strong antibiotic. Following her advice, I took a tablet. The doctor at my local health clinic back home had firmly warned me not to take Cipro for more than two days in a row, since it is a powerful drug. So I made a decision to not take the rest of the dosage, figuring I would need it even more on the trek.

After I arrived back at the hotel, I went online and communicated with Faith via Instant Messenger for a few minutes. It was fantastic chatting with her, half way around the world. I miss her already, although she'd never believe it.

Faith was very excited for me to go on this trip. She did a great deal of research on Nepal, much more than I did. Unfortunately, Faith has Raynaud's disease, a condition that is typically characterized as "being allergic to cold weather." The condition can cause pain within the affected extremities, as well as discoloration and numbness. Trekking in the frigid Himalayas would be too risky for her. Besides, even though I would love Faith to go trekking with me – anywhere – she doesn't enjoy it. She is healthy and stays fit in other ways, but trekking isn't her cup of tea. It used to bother me, but I've learned to accept it.

I returned to the room at 10:00 P.M. and packed the rest of my gear. I'm now ready for bed. Tomorrow is a big day.

What the Travel Brochure should have said for Days 1-4:

Day 1-4: NEW YORK TO KATHMANDU • 4,383 feet

Travel from your homeport to Kathmandu. Take four long, mind-numbing flights. You won't sleep much since you will be terribly jet-lagged. If you're already sick, you're going to get sicker. Long plane rides are perfect environments for germs to spread. When you finally arrive into Kathmandu, you'll check into a classic four-star hotel, based on Kathmandu standards, which is equal to a two star hotel in the U.S. You'll experience exotic food from all over the world, but it won't sit well with you. You'll shit your brains out. We'll then take you to some tourist destinations, some of them fascinating, but you won't be able to enjoy them since your health will be deteriorating. A favorite destination is the Monkey Temple, but you may be nauseated by the whole experience. Monkeys here, monkeys there, monkeys everywhere. Gross. Your adventure is just beginning. Fasten your seatbelt.

2

REPULSIVE

"...there ain't no journey what don't change you some."

-David Mitchell

11-11-04

TRAVEL BROCHURE DESCRIPTION:

Day 5: PHADKING • 8,700 feet

We fly on a twin-engine Otter to the Himalayan foothills where we will begin our trek into the Khumbu region. The views from the plane are amazing, providing dramatic views of terraced hills and the distant Himalayan giants. After landing in the village of Lukla (9,350 feet) we will meet the rest of our staff and porters and trek for about two and a half hours to Phadking.

Trekking Company Menu*:

Lunch:
Lemon/Orange/Tang Juice
Butter Sandwich, Salad
Tuna Fish, Finger Chips/ Chips, Fresh Fruits
Staff will provide washing soap, dilute potassium/iodine mixed hot water and a towel for the refreshment.
Tea / Coffee / Biscuits

Dinner:
Vegetable Chow mein, Tomato sausage, Yak Steak,
Boil Tea / Coffee / Drinking hot chocolates
hot water and soap for washing hands and a towels

*Here (and throughout) I have reproduced the eccentric wording and spelling of the tour company menu, verbatim.

9:00 P.M., town of Phadking

A t this moment, I'm sick to my stomach. I've been in the bathroom, otherwise known as the "outhouse," four times in the past hour with awful diarrhea. I also made a liquid deposit at almost every outhouse along the trail today – and trust me, there were many. I was horrified when I stepped into the first one on the trail.

Each successive visit along the trail became exponentially more disgusting. If you can imagine the most deplorable, unsanitary conditions you've ever seen in a public bathroom, or better yet, a port-a-potty, and multiply it by a thousand, you may have a slight idea of what I'm trying to convey. It stunk beyond my wildest imagination – and the sight of it combined with the atrocious smell made it so much worse. There was crap everywhere. There was hay scattered all over the outhouse floors to prevent trekkers from slipping when stepping into shit, and as important, to attempt to mask the pervasive odor. It didn't work. It was repugnant. By comparison, a port-a-potty full to the brim with human waste would seem like a bathroom at a five-star hotel.

It's unfortunate that people on the trail don't take the care which I try to take when defecating here. As disgusting as it sounds, they end up crapping all over the floor. It's terribly inconsiderate. One would think they would have the common courtesy toward their fellow human beings but, unfortunately, it's not the case. Regardless, I had to maneuver through an obstacle course of feces, with surgical precision, in order to not step in any of it while trying to get into the right squatting position.

It's a good thing I have strong quadriceps muscles, since as I mentioned the other day, toilets don't exist. I had to squat way down low to the floor in order to make sure my feces went through the approximately nine-inch hole in the center of each outhouse. If I wasn't meticulously careful with my targeting, I would have ended up defecating on myself since my feces basically consisted of pure liquid and would have splashed everywhere. Worse yet, I had to do all of this while holding my breath. If I attempted to breathe inside of the outhouse, I would have gagged and lost it. I used my jacket to conceal the smell as much as possible. I also needed to be extremely careful wiping myself, in order to not get crap on my clothes. This is much, much easier said than done while squatting for a couple of minutes, with my pants scrunched up around my legs and wearing lots of gear.

I have a limited amount of clothes with me, which need to last for the next two weeks, so I must attempt to keep them clean for as long as possible. There aren't any laundromats on the mountain.

I now understand why it was suggested I get immunized for tetanus, Hepatitis A, typhoid and meningitis prior to arriving here. These outhouses and the accompanying filth are prime hot spots for the spread of infectious diseases.

Why am I being so detailed in my description of these outhouses? It's because for the rest of my life, I never want to live through this again. I'm hoping I will read this journal in the future and avoid repeating this absolutely nightmarish experience. If I don't document it, I most certainly will forget it, since time generally heals all wounds. In the words of George Santayana, "those who cannot remember the past are condemned to repeat it."

As bad as it was today, I was fortunate that we were at a low altitude and it therefore wasn't too cold yet, so I wasn't wearing too many layers of clothes. More layers will make it much more difficult to relieve myself as we ascend. It's going to be quite a challenge when I'm in my full winter gear at higher altitudes.

I've also had a headache for the past few hours. I took aspirin, but it didn't help. Lorraine told me it was because I didn't drink enough water. She said it was imperative that I keep drinking all day long, in order to counteract the effects of the altitude. I was surprised to hear this, since I drank almost two liters today, but she said I should be drinking at least three, and closer to five, liters per day. I don't see how that's possible. If I drank five liters I wouldn't be able to hike at all since I'd be urinating constantly.

Lorraine also said my pee should be crystal clear. If it's not, then it's a signal I'm not drinking enough. I'm already concerned about drinking the water here, since the rivers are highly contaminated. During the monsoon season, human and animal waste left on the trails is washed into the rivers. Intestinal parasites, like giardia, among plenty of other diseases, abound, ready to prey on human hosts.

The trekking company supplies us with "treated" water. They use a heavy-duty, industrial-sized water filter to "attempt" to prevent any bacteria from passing through it. In addition, the water is treated with iodine, which is supposed to kill 99.9% of the bacteria. However, there are no guarantees. There are some bacteria which iodine cannot destroy. As long as the slightest bit of bacteria ends up getting past the water filter or survives the iodine treatment, and ultimately remains in the water you're drinking, you're screwed. And equally as bad, too much iodine in your body is not a good thing. It has been proven to cause significant health issues. So, it's either death by dysentery or death by iodine…or both.

Anyway, as sick as I am right now, I'm going to do my best to attempt to give you a full summary of today's events …

We left our hotel in Kathmandu at 6:30 AM. I couldn't sleep at all last night. I was completely wired, so I was glad to get an early start. We arrived at a rinky-dink air terminal around 7:00 A.M. Tribhuvan International airport is where all flights arrive into Kathmandu and from where all the small propeller planes fly to Lukla. Although the terminal was part of an international airport, it sure didn't seem like one.

Lukla is the standard starting point for most people beginning their treks in the Everest region. Lukla airport (otherwise known as Tenzing – Hillary Airport), at 9,200 feet and named after the first two individuals to summit Mt. Everest, is considered *the most* dangerous airport in the world. This is due to the altitude, the almost constant high winds, the cloud coverage, and the continuously changing visibility. There have been quite a few plane crashes over the past couple of decades flying into Lukla, with many fatalities. We were flying on Yeti Airlines, which has had its fair share of accidents. The fact that the airline was named after the cryptid ape-like "Abominable Snowman" of the Himalayas was not comforting either.

It was a mob scene at the airport. I have travelled through untold numbers of crowded airports in the past, many which seemed chaotic, but it was always "organized" chaos. There wasn't even the semblance of organization today. Huge crowds clamored for their chance to get near the front of the pack, like traders in the pit of the commodities exchange. I had no idea what was happening, but we fortunately had Lorraine to help us navigate through the insanity, since she speaks Nepali. Watching her take charge was like watching a master tactician. She was speaking fluently as if it were her native tongue, and she was also cleverly outmaneuvering plenty of guys much larger than she, who were trying to get the ticket agent's attention. She successfully took care of everything in a much shorter time than I would have believed possible, after seeing the initial commotion. She displayed impressive intelligence and resourcefulness. I felt reassured that she will be guiding us up the mountain.

Unfortunately, we had to wait three hours for our flight because our antiquated plane had mechanical problems. I was in Kathmandu, about to get on a plane operated by an airline with a joke of a name, and one that I've been informed isn't capable of flying. Yet strangely enough, when they finally fixed the mechanical defect, I didn't hesitate to climb aboard. To some degree, I just wanted to escape the craziness at the airport. But beyond that immediate desire, I realized there are going to be plenty of instances on this trek where I need to put my trust, and my life, in other people's hands, or more important, in the Lord's hands. This was just the first of many. Although I'm not a very religious person, I do occasionally find myself asking God to watch over me in dangerous situations, as I most certainly did today. I think I'll be doing this often over the next two weeks.

We finally took off for a forty-five minute flight to Lukla, in the Himalayas. The rumble of the engine and the lift-off surprisingly provided me with an instant, Zen-like peace, knowing I had just left the commotion and hustle-bustle of the big city of Kathmandu and was now headed toward serenity in the mountains.

Unfortunately, we couldn't see out of the passenger windows at all. They were entirely scratched up from years of wear and tear. We were able to get a slight peek through the pilot's window, since the cockpit door was unexpectedly left open.

Based on the little we could glimpse through the pilots' front window, it was a glorious view. The Himalayas appeared way off in the distance. Snow-covered mountains covered the entire horizon. They grew larger and more stunning as we flew closer and closer. I was overjoyed knowing I would be hiking in the midst of all this beauty within a few hours. There aren't many things more satisfying and rewarding than walking among some of this planet's most beautiful sights, while ultimately pushing one's body to its limit.

I wanted to take some pictures of the mountains from inside of the plane, but I couldn't because my camera was inside my backpack, which was resting on my lap. I could barely move my arms and legs because we were all crammed into the plane without an inch to maneuver in any direction. Jack was holding a large crate of eggs on his lap, Teddy was surrounded by unsecured cases of beer piled up all around him, and the rest of us had our backpacks and loads of other supplies sitting on top of our laps. The plane had run out of room in the luggage compartment, because they were transporting supplies to Lukla, so the overflow of goods was shifted into the passenger compartment. We couldn't budge, although there really wasn't any reason to since there wasn't a bathroom on the plane. Quite thankfully, my stomach was behaving for the moment. If it hadn't been, I surely would have been in dire straits.

I wondered what would happen if the National Transportation and Safety Board decided to do an inspection of the safety standards on our flight. There was no flight attendant or safety tutorial prior to takeoff or even any safety instructions in a seat pocket. After having been on close to a thousand flights the past couple of decades, this one certainly felt odd.

It really didn't matter that there were no safety instructions since if the plane ran into trouble, we were all dead. The lack of a seatbelt was the least of my worries. I was imagining the headlines in the papers back home, "Small plane crashes on Mt. Everest, thirteen Americans, 1 Spaniard, 1 Brit, and 2 Nepalese pilots all presumed dead. Bodies cannot be recovered due to remote location and will remain on mountain frozen in time forever."

Sadly, as I was working on this book in the fall of 2012, a plane bound for Lukla crashed after departing from Kathmandu. There were no survivors. There have been many other accidents since my trek, with two of them resulting in the deaths of all passengers on board.

I was surprisingly calm for most of the flight, especially considering I'm claustrophobic. I couldn't move, so I just tried to accept the fact that I might as well try to relax. "Breathe, David, breathe…long, slow, deep breaths."

We finally landed in Lukla and de-planed, we looked down the hill and couldn't believe our eyes. Nestled in between huge mountains was this miniscule airport. We had landed on a small stretch of airstrip, maybe a few hundred yards long, built right into the mountainside. I realized right then and there that it will be better for me to not think too much about what has just happened, or what will be happening, and instead, just go with the flow.

There was no arrival area to go through after we landed. There was a small building for departing passengers, but we didn't enter it. We simply grabbed our duffel bags, gathered the full team, and walked right off the runway to a teashop fifty yards away. Because our flight had been delayed in Kathmandu, we were running very late. We needed to get to Phadking (the "d" is silent, so it's pronounced "focking," which amused us all.)

We had a fifteen-minute lunch in Lukla at the tea lodge, which had a small dining area. It was surprisingly charming. I knew that we would pass many tea lodges and teashops along the trails, but most certainly nothing as large and nice as the one today. I had read that these small structures serve a limited number of drinks and refreshments. The typical limited fare in a Himalayan teashop, also referred to as a tea house, is hot tea, soda, Snickers, Pringles and beer. They exist to provide some warmth, a place for people to socialize, and occasionally, offer a few rooms for trekkers to sleep for the night. This lodge in particular had a sizeable dining room, enough for thirty people or so, or two separate trekking groups. The perimeter, bench-style seating was made of a polished, brown, tan, and orange-colored wood and gave the feeling we were inside of a small, rustic chalet. Looking through the large windows on all sides of us, the views of the airport, the incoming planes and the mountainside were fantastic.

We were served tiny, triangular finger sandwiches consisting of a small piece of cheese, a razor thin slice of tomato, and a teeny-weeny piece of onion, along with a few specks of canned tuna fish. They also provided some cold French fries and a frightening-looking cabbage dish resembling coleslaw, which was what they simply called "salad." I passed on the cabbage. Although I don't typically eat French fries, I ate a few for the carbs.

During lunch, the beverage choices offered by the trekking company were, and apparently always will be, powdered sugar juice, hot tea, coffee, or water. Fanta Orange soda was available for purchase at the tea lodge, so I purchased a can. I would come to enjoy many cans of Fanta orange soda on the trail, which was fine with me, as I love the stuff.

The teashop also offered beer and other forms of alcohol for purchase, but I don't drink beer, hardly ever drink wine, and never drink hard spirits. We met our porters and Sherpas, more than a dozen of them, and off we went.

If you haven't read or heard about Sir Edmund Hilary's conquest of Mount Everest accompanied by his Sherpa guide, Tenzing, you might not know much about the Sherpas of the Himalayas. Sherpas are an ethnic group from the high mountainous regions of Nepal, who migrated from Tibet hundreds of years ago. The use of the term Sherpa also generally refers to an elite guide, mountaineer, or climber, knowledgeable in the local terrain. My reference to Sherpas throughout this story will be of the climbing guides. Some Sherpa guides are not necessarily of Sherpa ethnicity, but those on our trek were, as were the porters.

There were no roads or streets in Lukla, only a single trail, composed of dirt and rock, which ran for about one half-mile right through the center of town east to west along its length. The airport was located on the eastern edge of town. The hiking trail basically began once we left the airport, and headed west, but the official start of the trail began on the western edge of town. The tiny village of Lukla was divided in half by the trail, splitting the northern and southern portions. Since the town is literally built into the mountainside, there weren't many buildings anywhere except for those hugging and bordering the trail. There were a limited number of farms adjacent to the airport runway, but otherwise, there were only teashops and tiny stores.

The start of the hike reminded me of the scene from the movie *The Ten Commandments* when the Jews were getting ready to leave Egypt with everything they owned. There were hundreds of trekkers, Sherpas, and porters packing up gear, loading duffels on their backs, preparing to hike up the trail. There were plenty more trekkers arriving in Lukla from higher up the trail, returning home after long journeys. The trekking season had started a few weeks earlier. The monsoon season runs from June through mid-October. Once it ends, trekking season kicks into full swing.

There were dozens of yaks and dzos spread throughout the town along the trail. A dzo is a hybrid of a yak and a cow. They were carrying the largest and heaviest gear, including the duffels, tents, cooking supplies, some food, and much more. There were trekkers from all over the world. I heard at least a dozen different languages being spoken as I walked past different trekking groups getting ready to begin their journeys. There were Sherpas gathering their groups and getting ready to guide their teams out of Lukla and up to Phadking, Namche Bazaar, and beyond.

The town of Lukla, which probably has a population of a few hundred people at most, was buzzing with activity amongst the trekkers, merchants, and townspeople. The merchants – mothers, fathers, grandparents, or kids – were aggressively accosting every trekker, trying to sell their wares. They were pushing handcrafted items, hiking gear, hats, souvenirs, food, candy, soda, and other items. I imagine I could have found almost any basic necessity if I looked hard enough, yet I was pretty sure I had everything I needed. I had made sure that I had gathered every single item on the suggested list of gear before I departed.

There were children returning from their school day and there were mobs of adolescents begging for money, or whatever else they could get from the relatively rich foreigners. We all wanted to give them something, yet we had nothing to give just yet. We were starting out on our journey and we brought along only what we thought we would absolutely need on the trek, and nothing more. Even though we did have money to give, we thought handing over cash at that moment would have resulted in a flock of kids following us all the way up to Phadking and beyond. So we resisted the temptation, thinking we could be more generous, especially with the gear, upon our return.

We walked past cinderblock storefronts and brightly painted teashops, one after the other, for a half-mile, before the shops ultimately disappeared. Then, we passed a handful of small homes and tiny farms on the southern side of the trail, and a few tiny, skillfully constructed homes built right into the mountain face on the northern side – until the homes too, vanished from sight.

All along the trail to Phadking, there were scores of porters passing us in each direction. We were moving at a reasonable pace, but we managed to stop to take a couple of pictures. There were additional teashops and outhouses spread throughout the winding path. We were informed that over the next couple of weeks, we would pass scores of teashops along the trails, although they would obviously be fewer and farther between the higher we ascend.

It took us three hours to get to Phadking. The scenery was absolutely beautiful, very similar to many places I've hiked in the U.S. with tall evergreens, heavy brush, flowing rivers and lush, green forest all around us. And there were tall peaks on the outskirts. As long as we weren't hiking near an outhouse, we could smell the sweet scents of nature.

We were still way below the tree line today, the edge of the habitat where trees are capable of growing. Above the tree line, the weather conditions are too harsh for trees and most plants to survive. Vegetation was flourishing everywhere, since the fields aren't as exposed to the cold weather and the high winds as they are at higher altitudes.

We couldn't enjoy the scenery as much as we would have liked since we were trying to get to Phadking before sunset – which we barely managed to do. So instead of being able to relish the views or even having a chance to interact with the locals, we had to move quickly down into the valley towards Phadking. Since we were hiking at a rapid pace, I had to keep my head down, in order to see the ground directly in front of my feet. The actual trail was just a dirt path, but with plenty of loose, small stones and baseball-sized rocks being kicked forward – some by accident and some on purpose by trekkers just kicking them for the heck of it. Either way, as insignificant as they were, the rocks created real dangers, since they could potentially cause the trekkers to trip and fall, sprain an ankle, or worse. So we needed to be constantly aware of what was in front of us.

The bigger risks, and causes of many injuries when trekking, are the larger, jagged, bowling ball-sized boulders that are deeply embedded in the dirt trail. They are unfortunately, similar to an iceberg, only partially exposed. It would only take a split second of not paying attention for me to catch my hiking boot against the immovable object, causing me to fall flat on my face. It probably wouldn't be catastrophic, unless there happened to be an additional boulder in the spot where my face happened to land.

Most of the trek today was downhill, since we landed in Lukla at 9,200 feet and descended down to Phadking at 8,700 feet. This is a very important fact and something I never gave any real thought to before arriving here. This entire trek is going to involve constant ascending and descending, over rivers and past hills and valleys, day after day, for the next two weeks. It's not at all like hiking a fourteener (mountains over 14,000 feet) in Colorado, contrary to what I had very mistakenly expected. There are over fifty peaks in Colorado over 14,000 feet. I've hiked a few of them and they've all (generally) required a relatively steady incline and straight climb, via switchbacks, to the summit. This trek is going to be different and much more challenging, because of these "ups and downs." Besides dealing with the altitude increases, I'll be working two or three times harder than I expected, since I'll constantly be ascending and descending, and then ascending some more. I hope I'm ready for this – I'm not sure if I've prepared enough.

The same can't be said for the Nepalese porters, however. They are fully prepared and are amazingly fit. It's extraordinary how much weight a porter can carry up these trails. Most porters carry 30 kilos, which is approximately 66 pounds, but some will carry as much as 60 kilos or more. According to one of my Sherpas, it's not that unusual for a porter to carry 100 kilos, or 220 pounds -- about the same weight a yak will typically carry. Their loads are supported by a naamlo, which is a strap of cloth that is wrapped around the forehead. The strap helps hold their gear in place, evenly supporting it and providing a center of gravity. I can't imagine the kind of headaches they must have at the end of a long trekking day.

A porter is paid by the kilo. An average payment to bring thirty kilos to Namche Bazaar at 11,300 feet is only 300 rupees, or approximately $4.25. The trip to Namche is a long, hard day and a half of backbreaking work. I'm sure there are plenty of porters who rush to do it in a day, rather than a day and a half, since they get paid by the job, not by the hour. Porters have to be some of the most underpaid, yet hard-working and fittest people on the planet. And amazingly, most of them are quite small. To my North American eyes, they look like kids. I wouldn't be shocked if some of them are just kids, although the trekking company told us otherwise. Most of them only average five feet or so in height, and routinely carry more than their own weight in gear. If there were ever an Olympic event that measured pure endurance combined with brute strength, pound for pound, I think the Nepalese porters would win hands down. On top of all of this, being a Sherpa or porter is undoubtedly one of the most dangerous jobs in the world – not so much so prior to base camp, but most certainly beyond it toward the summit of Everest.

Whenever a porter is walking with a heavy load, you need to let him, *or her*, pass. (Yes, there are many female porters. There are equal rights here, at least when it comes to carrying heavy burdens up the side of a mountain. They carry cases of beer on their backs, boxes of supplies, building materials, and more, just like the men.) In all probability, the porters will be carrying a massive amount of weight, panting and sweating profusely, as if they had just run a marathon. You can't help but feel for them as they go by. And as small as they are, they make you feel even smaller when you realize the hard work they do every day of their lives, compared to what most of us do – or at least compared to what many of my friends and associates and I do.

Although there were a number of porters accompanying us on the trek today, many more of them were simply transporting goods up and down the mountain, mostly back and forth between Lukla and Namche Bazaar. They will carry anything that can fit on their backs.

Porters generally come from the lower altitudes in the Himalayas. Many are poor farmers looking for extra income. Utilizing porters to move goods is basically one of two methods of facilitating the flow of commerce here, no different from the air, rail, and trucking industries back in the U.S. It's not feasible or economical, and certainly not safe, to use advanced methods of transport to move goods here. The narrow, rocky, and steep trails will not accommodate vehicles of any kind, and it is way too dangerous to fly in, or helicopter in, supplies higher up in the mountains. Helicopters are, in fact, used quite often in emergencies to air-evacuate sick or injured climbers, but the cost is prohibitive for most other uses.

The other mode of transporting goods is via a yak or a dzo. Yaks are uniquely adapted to high altitude. They are large, strong, and possess unique red blood cells that allow them to take in more oxygen than typical cattle. Their heavy coats enable them to survive in cold weather. Yaks are the freight trains of the Himalayas, carrying all of the heaviest and most cumbersome gear and supplies.

As I mentioned earlier, moving aside for a porter is the "considerate" thing to do, but getting out of the way of a passing yak is an absolute necessity if you want to live. Yaks and dzos on the trail are like slowly moving tanks. Tanks have cannons to kill, and yaks have daunting, mammoth horns – like those of a bull – that can effectively accomplish the same job.

A slow moving trekker is a minor impediment to a yak. Therefore, we need to be constantly on alert for what might be heading toward us or coming up from behind, which won't be easy to do while we're exhausted from hiking. It's easy to become careless, as well as oblivious to our surroundings, if we're tired from hours of trekking.

Oftentimes, we'll be moving more slowly than the yaks and will most definitely be in their path. If a yak gets close to us while we're trekking, we will have no choice but to let it pass, no matter how we do it. And we will need to do it quickly. The smart option generally is to stand on the higher, northern side of the trail, facing into the mountain, versus standing on the south side of the trail, which in most cases translates into standing on the edge of a cliff. If we don't move fast enough, we can get gored, or possibly worse, depending on your preferred method of demise, get shoved off the edge of the cliff.

At many points along the trail, a drop can be a few hundred feet or more. According to Lorraine, it will not be unusual to see one thousand foot drops along the trail as we gain altitude, and the trails will also be narrower, leaving less room for the yaks to maneuver. She warned us never to attempt to pass the yaks on the trail, since they really don't care if they happen to bump us, step on us, or gore us. The better bet is to just be patient, enjoy our surroundings, and do our best to stay alive. We can always wait until the yaks stop somewhere for a rest before we try to pass.

Don't pass the yaks – just get out of their way.

In addition to the porters, there are seven Sherpas with us. They are also in great shape and are going to be our guides and caretakers during this trek. One Sherpa leads the group, one trails the group, and the others spread out amongst the team. They will alternate their positions each day. They're all wonderful guys. Most of them got their jobs by being a friend of one of the other Sherpas, or by being related to a local employee of the trekking company. Our crew consisted of all sorts of relatives – uncles, cousins, brother-in-laws, etc. – of the local manager of the trekking company. Here is a real example of the importance of knowing people in "high places."

Being a Sherpa is much easier work, physically, than being a porter. A Sherpa guides us up the mountain, and may carry an extra backpack for a day or two. The porters do the heavy work, with the goal of proving themselves worthy, over time, to be hired as a Sherpa. In addition to the seven Sherpas, we have eight porters, a cook with a kitchen staff of ten, and twelve yaks to carry our duffels and all of the supplies necessary to make our trip somewhat comfortable and manageable.

The group dynamics were interesting today. Since there are only fifteen people on the trek including the two guides, I was interested in developing a rapport with at least a few members of the team. I attempted to hike with most everyone at different points throughout the afternoon, my goal being to simply converse with them and get to know them a bit.

I first hiked with George and Randy. George is very talkative, a great guy with a warped sense of humor. He and I are getting along great. He is the only person out of the thirteen on our trek who also has young kids, so we have lots of things in common to discuss. I think it's strange that there aren't more people my age who are married with kids. Then again, I guess there aren't many men, or women, in my position who can afford to go away for three weeks and have their spouse be comfortable with it. Maybe those individuals are just smart enough to know not to go on a trek like this, whether to avoid the pain and misery of being in the Himalayas for two weeks, or to avoid the repercussions from their spouses when they return home.

Unfortunately, I couldn't get a word out of Randy at all. I'm not sure if he has no interest in making new friends or if he is just an intensely private and quiet guy. He's a truly large brute and, because he's so quiet, he's a bit intimidating. I wonder what's going on inside his head.

Teddy and Mitch are very friendly and seem open to getting to know me, and vice versa. Robin and Kim have already bonded since they are the only two women on the team, besides the two guides, and they are both single. Jack and Ian were way ahead of the pack for most of the day, so I wasn't able to speak with them. I typically hike at a decent pace, especially when I'm going downhill, but they were moving unbelievably quickly and were way ahead of the rest of the group. So I ended up speaking with Jay, Fernando, and John for much of the time – the only three guys who had come on the trip without a friend or close companion. They are all single, although I think Jay and John are both divorced or separated from their wives.

When we finally arrived at Phadking, the porters were in the process of setting up our tents, which were supposed to have been ready for occupancy by the time we arrived at the camp site. However, since this was the first day of our trek, they didn't get a head start on us. I finally made it into my tent late in the afternoon, washed up, and then headed to dinner in the tea lodge. We ate dinner at dusk in the glass-enclosed sunroom of the tea lodge.

Although I was starving since I hadn't eaten many of the "finger" sandwiches at lunch, and I had also been hiking all afternoon, I ate very little for dinner. The kitchen staff served yak steak, chow mein, hash browns, and soup. I didn't touch the yak steak – for multiple reasons. My stomach had been shaky all day. It was also difficult to get comfortable with the concept of eating yak meat considering I was hiking with yaks throughout the day. (More to the point, however, the sight of it nauseated me.) And, I had also read somewhere that there was a "no-kill" policy on the mountain with regards to the yaks, which meant that the meat brought along on our trek would get older, and therefore much less desirable, with each passing day. I wasn't sure if this was true or not, but I felt comfortable not asking anyone, in order to justify my decision to not eat red meat on the mountain. I also avoided the chow mein. Chow mein typically looks pretty threatening in a clean, reputable Chinese restaurant back home. It looked deadly here.

The persistent cough I've had kept acting up all day, so I thought soup would be a smart and safe thing to have. It was boiling hot, so I convinced myself that any dangerous microorganisms had been killed. Although it scorched my tongue and the roof of my mouth as I chugged it down, it felt healing and soothing to my sore throat.

Considering both the outside temperature and my average body temperature were dropping minute-by-minute on the mountain, the soup gave my body a brief reprieve from the cold. I ate a forkful of hash brown potatoes, but it was a struggle getting them down my ailing throat.

I should be eating as much as possible, since I'm supposed to be overdosing on carbohydrates. I need to create fuel for my body for all of the hiking I'm going to be doing every day. However, since I am devoid of sleep, dehydrated from intestinal disease, and fatigued from the hiking earlier in the day, I have no desire to eat. This is apparently quite typical at high altitudes and is clearly not just an issue for me. Others in the group didn't feel like eating either. It oddly gave me a slight sense of companionship that they were feeling similarly ill. Misery does love company.

After dinner, I returned to the tent. It's late in the evening now. I need to be extremely careful going to the outhouse, which is about thirty yards away from my tent, by the riverside. It's easy to get hurt because there are large boulders everywhere. I've been there four times already, so I fortunately know my way around the landmines – both outside the outhouse and within.

What the Travel Brochure should have said:

Day 5: PHADKING • 8,700 feet

We fly on a twin-engine Otter, one of a few which miraculously hasn't yet crashed, into the Himalayan foothills. You'll be terrified for your life, but it will be an amazing experience, assuming you land safely. The views from the antiquated plane are astounding, providing you can see through the worn windows. After landing in the charming village of Lukla, you will meet the amazing staff and trek to Phadking. Along the way, you'll quickly learn to stay alive by dodging yaks and porters. You will be absolutely nauseated by the horrific outhouses, as you visit nearly each and every one of them. However, you'll also be very lucky today, because you'll be descending to Phadking – an easy hike. You won't be so lucky for the next ten days. So brace yourself. Oh, and be prepared to starve. Regardless of what is on the menu, you'll probably eat very little today, tomorrow, and everyday thereafter.

3

SELF-DOUBT

"Every step you take is a step away from where you used to be."

-Brian Chargualaf

11-12-04

TRAVEL BROCHURE DESCRIPTION:

Day 6: NAMCHE BAZAAR • 11,300 feet

We continue trekking along the banks of the Dudh Kosi, crossing this majestic river many times on exciting suspension bridges laden with prayer flags. After entering Sagamartha National Park, the trail climbs steeply with breathtaking views to Namche Bazaar, the gateway to the Khumbu region.

Trekking Company Menu:

Wakeup tea/ Coffee/ Hot Chocolates

B/F:
Porridge, Omlet, Toast Bread
Tea / Coffee / Hot Chocolate

Lunch:
Juice, Black tea
French Toast, Vinegar dressing Salad, Sardine Fish, Sote
Fried Potatoes
Tea / Coffee/ Chocolates

Refreshment
Tea / Coffee / Chocolates with Biscuits and snacks

Dinner:
Mixed soup, Nepalese Dish, Green vegetables, Desert
Cauliflower, Potato Bread, fruits
Tea / Coffee / Drinking Hot Chocolates

6:00 P.M., town of Namche Bazaar

W hat a "Phadking" day. It was a real grind getting ready this morning. I was feeling decidedly "under the weather" thanks to my assorted maladies and having only slept three hours last night. My sick stomach and a constant need to urinate because of all the water I am drinking kept me running to the outhouse all night. My leg muscles were tight and my body was sore from the trekking yesterday. I had to force myself out of the sleeping bag knowing it was wickedly cold outside. I reluctantly acknowledged I had no choice.

The only real incentive for getting out of my "cocoon" – my warm, comfortable, snug sleeping bag – was that I knew I'd be having some boiling hot water to drink in order to warm my internal organs. Instead of having "room service" here, the porters provide "tent service" each morning. Today, they approached my tent at 7:00 A.M. and loudly announced "Good morning Mr. David. It is time to wake up." Of course, I had been awake for hours. They served coffee and tea, but I asked for hot water. I don't drink coffee or anything caffeinated, and they didn't have decaf tea. I wisely had brought my own decaf teabags.

The porters also poured me a large bowl of hot water for washing myself and brushing my teeth. I purposely left the bowl outside of the tent. It would be all too easy to accidentally knock the bowl over and spill it all over my gear, which was spread out throughout the tent. If my gear gets wet, it will be useless for the next two weeks. The tent is tight – probably seven-feet long by five-feet wide or so at the base and forms a triangle at the top, almost four feet at its highest point. I can't stand upright in the tent, since I'm six feet tall, but I fortunately have a few inches of clearance above my head if I'm sitting down.

Initially, I thought brushing my teeth was a hassle. However, it turned out to be quite simple relative to the effort required to wash myself. First, I have to strip down to my underwear, allowing the sub-freezing air to hit every inch of my exposed skin. If undressing in a virtual icebox isn't bad enough, the washing is even worse. Even though the water is steaming hot when the porter delivers it to me, it doesn't take more than a minute or so to cool off and then become ice-cold as it is exposed to the frigid air. It certainly does a great job of waking me up. I have to be a contortionist to reach out of the tent flap for some water, ensuring the rag doesn't leak on my gear, and then move quickly to wash, and then wipe myself dry, body-part by body-part.

I then have to get dressed and organize my gear for the day. Not surprisingly, even the most basic tasks at home become major, physical efforts here. The altitude makes any task more strenuous. All of my clothes are divided among different Hefty liners (plastic trash bags), by type of garment. I did this at the recommendation of the trekking company, in order to keep everything dry and organized. The duffel bag will constantly be exposed to moisture for much of the day since it sits on top of a yak for seven hours or so, while it possibly rains and snows. The duffel isn't waterproof, so I need to protect the gear inside by packing it all in those plastic liners.

Thus, in order to dress in the morning, I need to untie every bag, take out my socks from one bag, pants from another, shirts from another and so on. (If I had everything in one liner bag, it would be way too messy, and the bag would also tear easily.) Then I need to line up everything in an orderly fashion. And of course this all has to be done prior to stripping down and washing myself, or I'd freeze my naked ass off while figuring it all out.

Once I am finally dressed, but prior to breakfast, I also have to pack up all of my sleeping gear. This includes the onerous tasks of rolling up my sleeping bag so tightly that it fits snugly into a miniscule sleeping bag sack, as well as compressing and rolling up my pillows so they fit into stuff-sacks one quarter their size. Once each item is rolled up, I have to sit on it to keep it compressed, and then quickly stuff them into their respective sacks. This actually takes a great deal of effort in the high altitude air. After the sleeping gear is packed airtight, I then have to tie all of the other liner bags, but only after squeezing all of the air out of them as well. Then, all of the bags need to be strategically placed in the duffel bag. Ultimately, everything has to fit perfectly, like the pieces of a three-dimensional puzzle.

We are required to fully pack our duffel in the morning and then put it outside of our tent before breakfast. The porters then take the duffels while we are eating breakfast and load them on to the yaks, and they immediately depart for the next campsite. We thus don't have access to our duffel bag during the entire day while we are trekking. This means I also have to prepare the contents of my backpack for the day, before closing the duffel.

The contents of my backpack will differ each day, depending on the weather forecast, so it requires some careful planning each morning. As it gets colder, I will need to have more layers with me – mostly as a precaution. So I must have this all figured out and have the appropriate gear already in my backpack before the porters depart with the duffels. If I don't get it right, I could be in trouble if the weather worsens.

This entire morning ritual takes close to an hour. By the time it is done, I am terribly winded, and I haven't even started trekking yet! I'm well aware it's going to get progressively worse each morning as we gain altitude.

For breakfast, we were served lukewarm eggs, hard toast and hot oatmeal. I had no appetite. I nibbled on a small piece of cold, hard toast with peanut butter and jam, and I also had some oatmeal. It's amazing how eggs here can seem so unappetizing considering I generally love eating eggs at home, but I guess even the most desirable foods can seem unappealing when you're not feeling well (although I certainly wouldn't consider the eggs they served today as resembling anything close to "desirable.") The altitude also is an appetite suppressant, which is highly unfortunate, since we actually should be eating *more* calories than normal for our strenuous hiking in the thin air.

After breakfast, we started out on an incredibly physically demanding day, hiking along the banks of the Dudh Kosi, the river that drains the Mount Everest massif and ultimately exits Sagarmatha National Park. (Sagarmatha is the Nepalese name for Mount Everest.) We crossed the river a few times on a number of simple suspension bridges. My knowledge of suspension bridges up until now was mostly limited to San Francisco's Golden Gate, but these bridges had nothing in common with that modern-day wonder. Most of the bridges here are one to two hundred feet long and are made of rope and steel cable with wooden planks. They seem terribly old and highly unsafe, although we were assured by Lorraine that all of the bridges here are, in fact, quite secure. The few that we crossed today shook uncontrollably as we walked across them, particularly when all of the other trekkers, yaks, porters and Sherpas did as well at the same time. We all thought the cables were going to snap based on the weight they were supporting, yet each time we successfully crossed one bridge, it gave us a little more confidence to cross the next.

We hiked alongside the river for almost three hours in the morning, through green forests, with the fragrant scent of the tall evergreens wafting on the breeze. Early in the morning we passed a number of farms, with hens and roosters scurrying about and chasing each other. Massive boulders, larger than many of the homes, were wedged into the walls of rock and dirt we passed, waiting hundreds or thousands of years to be loosened just enough to allow gravity to force their next move further south. I was praying that the actual timing of those moments wouldn't be while I happened to be walking immediately below them.

Hiking up to Phadking from Lukla. The homes and tea shops are rather small.

One of the many bridges we experienced...

...and another.

The more we walked, the less crowded the trail became. It was a generally comfortable morning with cool weather, beautiful views, and plenty of swaying bridges to traverse. Overall, I'd say I was operating at 50% of my optimal level. Typically, when I'm trekking, I feel like a million bucks. I have an attitude that leads me to believe I am invincible. However, if my body starts to deteriorate for any one of the multiple reasons I have mentioned here, my confidence level drops. Regardless from where the physical issues emanate, I begin to question my abilities and it becomes a vicious cycle of self-doubt.

We stopped for lunch around noon. Jack and Ian were waiting for us at the teashop when we arrived. They had ascended much earlier, in record time. Ian is in his early twenties, with a strong Irish accent, five-foot ten or so, husky, and extremely fit. He plays rugby back home. Jack is a handsome, athletic guy with a dirty-blonde crew-cut, who looks like a professional baseball player who is winding down his career. He must be 35 years old or so and is a social worker at a boys' school. Although the two of them didn't know each other prior to this trip, they seem to be best buddies already. I chalked up their easy intimacy to Jack's experience working with kids.

For lunch we had French toast, potatoes au gratin, green beans and coleslaw. I didn't watch the cooks prepare the food, but the veggies were clearly from cans. I probably would have enjoyed an MRE meal as much as what they served today, which clearly isn't saying much about the quality of the food here. The odd combination of food and seemingly random side dishes was only part of the problem. The tastelessness of the food was a major issue. The high altitude of the Himalayas just didn't seem to be the best place to enjoy the typical American comfort food favorites being served here. I wondered why we weren't being provided with dishes that were more typically Asian, if not authentically Nepalese — not that it would have mattered regardless, since I just didn't feel like eating anything. Just the same, I realized during lunch that I had to completely adjust my eating expectations for the next two weeks. I certainly didn't think I'd be having gourmet meals, of course, but I had hoped the food would be somewhat better. Whenever I've hiked in the past, I would always manage to bring along a few meals that always tasted great, particularly after a hard day of physical effort. I'm not a food snob by any means. I would eat pizza every day of my life, and dumplings of course, if it was up to me. Fortunately, Faith wouldn't allow this to happen. I nibbled on the French toast, as a bird might, but ultimately couldn't stomach it.

The hike after lunch was absolutely grueling. We had to climb 2,300 feet, on an extremely steep, challenging slope, up to Namche Bazaar. I started feeling worse, after not eating much for lunch. The temperature was dropping as the clouds rolled in. I was already worn-out from a lack of sleep and I was becoming worried about being able to summit in a week from now based on how I was feeling, and knowing that in all probability I was going to feel worse.

Lorraine wisely told us immediately after lunch that the best way to make it up to Namche Bazaar was by taking a single step, and then resting for a quick second, before taking another step. This is appropriately named the "rest" step. So that's what I did the entire way up, moving like a turtle and taking step after step – small ones, thousands, with a rest in between each and every one of them. Although I was physically and mentally exhausted after each and every step, I just kept on moving forward, constantly and robotically. My biggest incentive for doing so was being able to stay warm. Every time I attempted to rest for more than a few seconds, a terrible chill would rush through my body, since I was sweating profusely. The warm sweat on my skin, underneath all of my layers, turned cold in an instant from the low temperature and blowing winds if I stopped moving. So I reluctantly just kept marching forward.

The scenery today was very similar to yesterday – mostly forest. As we ascended, however, we started seeing more expansive views, higher up the mountains where the trees ceased to exist. The craggy mountain faces extended way off into the distance, making me aware of the vastness of the Himalayas. We were only in one large valley, and the Himalayas extend for almost 1,500 miles. We were still trekking way below the tree line and had been all day, but the few trees we did see were certainly sparser than those below us. Over the next few days, the higher we climb, the less we'll be seeing green and the more we'll be seeing gray and white – rock and snow.

All that said, I paid very little attention to the views during the afternoon. I was working my body so hard that it ultimately caused my mind to enter some sort of trance-like state. My brain detached itself from the entire situation – from the hike, my anxieties, and life in general. It blocked everything out except for the simple task of putting one foot in front of the other.

I've been in this "zone" other times in my life. They always happened when I've climbed very high-altitude mountains in the U.S., such as Mt. Elbert, Longs Peak, and Mt. Whitney, all mountains over 14,000 feet. During each of those climbs, I generally carried a forty-pound backpack loaded with my tent and gear. And each time, it felt like I was hauling a refrigerator on my back up the Empire State Building. I'd become physically exhausted around 10,000 feet, from the altitude and the physical effort. Every step I took above 12,000 feet felt like it was the last one I could possibly muster, as I gasped for whatever scant oxygen I could suck into my asthmatic lungs. Every muscle in my legs burned. To counter the exhaustion, my body went into "autopilot" mode. Although being utterly fatigued, I simply moved to the rhythm of my heavily beating heart. My brain would shut down all logic, which would otherwise tell me to stop and turn back. Maybe it was adrenaline telling me to fight instead of flee. Or maybe it was simply the fact that I wouldn't accept failure.

Miraculously, in spite of my slow-motion rest step, I arrived hours later into Namche Bazaar.

As I turned the page to continue writing, I discovered this note written in my journal.

11/5/04 Dear Daddy,
Wow, you're actually going, I can't believe it. I didn't even realize that you were leaving this sunday. I wonder if your on the mountain now. First when I started writing I didn't think that you would even see this entry from me. I had the idea of getting you the grapermelon gum. I really hope you don't get to jetlag that would really stink. To tell you the truth when we were in the car coming back from Jasmine, I was crying. but I just got to remember that this is what you really want to do and know. I understand that. I Really Really REALLY want you to have a good time and come home healthy. I ♡ YOU SO MUCH!!!!!! ALWAYS, love always

I love you. = J + ♡ + ☺ -Tori-

Tori, this letter meant so much to me. I really miss you sweetie.

59

10:00 P.M.

We were informed a little while ago that John has decided to go home. He's going back to Lukla in the morning. For some reason, he did not bring the appropriate gear with him and he isn't prepared for the trek. He is making the right decision. He foolishly wore blue jeans today. Wearing jeans when trekking is not smart in general, but wearing them in freezing temperatures is crazy. It can easily cause hypothermia. He must have realized when he arrived in Namche Bazaar that wearing cotton apparel of any kind in this environment was a huge mistake. His jeans were soaking wet from the long, strenuous hike. Once he stopped trekking, they probably started to freeze, and then his body did as well.

I didn't expect this from him. He had shown up the first day wearing a safari hat and one of those trekking shirts with multiple pockets to hold all sorts of gear. I pegged him as having the full lock, stock and barrel of appropriate supplies required to survive on this journey. Although he is close to fifty years old and showing his age, he seemed very knowledgeable about trekking. He clearly had me fooled.

Any person who treks on a regular basis knows you should never wear anything made from cotton since it absorbs moisture and doesn't dry. Not only does cotton not provide protection from the cold, it actually has the opposite effect and will make the situation worse. We were all given an extensive, detailed list of gear to bring with us. All of it needed to fit into one large duffel bag, with one significant limitation. The fully packed duffel was restricted to a maximum allowable weight of forty pounds, since there was a slight possibility a porter would need to carry it. Typically, the yaks carry the duffels. In the case of an emergency, however, the porters might have to carry them. Thus, before we started out on our hike when we arrived in Lukla, all of the duffels were weighed. If a bag was over the weight limit, as some were, items needed to be removed. And if this occurred, which it did with a few people, the contents of their duffels had to be completely taken apart in order to determine which items, of least importance, to eliminate.

Here's the list of gear we were instructed to bring, exactly as it was printed in our pre-trek packet:

1) *Good hiking boots, with a sturdy mid-sole and Vibram sole. Make sure you break them in well before the trip. If you don't, you'll have blisters after the first day.*
2) *Sneakers (I brought a hybrid sneaker/hiking shoe.)*
3) *Sandals*
4) *Gaiters (worn over the hiking boot and bottom half of the pants in order to prevent snow from getting inside and soaking your socks)*
5) *Down booties.*
6) *Few pairs of both and lightweight and heavy socks (synthetic or wool – not cotton.)*
7) *Lightweight and mid-weight long underwear tops (non-cotton)*
8) *Lightweight long underwear bottoms (non-cotton)*
9) *Mid-weight underwear bottom (non-cotton)*
10) *Four (or more) underwear briefs (synthetic or cotton)*
11) *Two short-sleeved cotton shirts and two synthetic short-sleeve shirts (athletic wear)*
12) *Synthetic or fleece jacket*
13) *Synthetic insulated pants*
14) *Down insulated jacket. A hood is optional and is highly recommended. (I brought two, a basic one as recommended, and also a heavy duty expedition parka, which I didn't expect to use but decided to bring just in case.)*
15) *Waterproof/breathable jacket with hood and pants, preferably with a side opening*
16) *Liner gloves (synthetic)*
17) *Windproof, fleece gloves.*
18) *Waterproof mittens*
19) *Two bandanas*
20) *Lightweight hat with good sun protection*
21) *Wool or fleece Hat*

22) *Balaclava (worn over the head and face to protect the face from cold winds)*

23) *Two pair of high quality 100% UV sunglasses (just in case you lose one)*

24) *Good quality headlamp w/ spare batteries and spare bulb*

25) *Backpack: 2500 cubic inches or more, internal frame.*

26) *Sleeping Bag: 30 Fahrenheit or better, preferably goose down with a 700 fill minimum*

27) *Two 1-liter, leak-proof, wide-mouth water bottles*

28) *One 1-liter, leak-proof wide-mouth pee bottle. Mark it clearly.*

29) *Pack towel*

30) *Trekking poles*

31) *Sun and lip screen, with a high SPF*

32) *Toiletry kit: toothbrush, toothpaste, lotion, alcohol-based anti-bacterial hand sanitizer, anti-bacterial soap, comb/brush, shave kit, lighter, small long-burning candle, needle/thread, throat lozenges, baby wipes, earplugs, and lots of toilet paper and tissues.*

33) *First aid kit: Ibuprofen/aspirin, assorted band aids, moleskin, little of hydrogen peroxide, Neosporin, small gauze pad, roll of adhesive tape, tweezers, safety pins. Prescription travel meds prescribed by your doctor (antibiotics, Diamox, malaria meds, sleep aids, etc.)*

34) *Large trash bags: For waterproofing your items*

35) *Zip-Loc bags, big and small*

36) *Water purification tablets or some other form of purification*

37) *Few stuff sacks for organizing your gear and clothes.*

38) *Pouch for your passport and valuables*

39) *Books to read*

40) *Journal*

41) *Camera with extra batteries*

42) *Duffel bag*

43) *Swiss army knife*

The above items are those the trekking company recommended. In addition to these items, I also brought along twenty Clif Bar energy bars (one for each day), a few packages of Gu, which is a carbohydrate gel, trail-mix, a few packages of candy, and a portable, lightweight chair for sitting in my tent.

In all, my total gear ended up weighing close to fifty-five pounds. However, I knew I'd be carrying a backpack, so I figured I'd carry the additional fifteen pounds on my back. I also figured that as we started the trek, I'd be eating into my stash of energy bars and trail mix and I would reduce the weight each day as we ascended.

I intended to give away almost all of my gear at the end of the trek. The Sherpas and porters all needed my gear more than I did. I brought to Nepal everything on the list above and I planned on returning home with only a few items – my backpack, my sleeping bag, my Northface shell, and a couple of other necessities.

One more thing I brought to Nepal was a foam pillow. I knew I wouldn't sleep well without it. I know everything you'd ever want to know about pillows, because I used to be in the pillow business. I worked for my father's company -- a down and feather business -- for six years, until I physically couldn't work there any longer because of my asthma and dust allergies.

Even with the pillow, there is still one significant difference which makes sleeping in a tent nothing like sleeping in a bed. In the tent, I have a one-inch thick rubber pad to sleep on (provided by the trekking company.) Although the pad offers some slight protection from the frozen ground, it is still terribly uncomfortable. If there are any rocks on the ground, even pebbles, I feel them, particularly the jagged ones sticking into my spine. Although the porters do their best to avoid any rough patches before they set up the tent, it is impossible to smooth out the rocky ground completely. After a long hard day of lugging heavy weight up the mountain, and as much as they absolutely tried their hardest to please us, the porters certainly weren't focused on finding a perfectly flat ground so I could get a good night's sleep.

After Lorraine told us about John heading home, she thought it would be a good time to also tell us about the dangers of high altitude illnesses. As lead guide, Lorraine is responsible for informing us of the dangers we face.

Altitude sickness*, also known as acute mountain sickness or AMS, is a pathological effect of high altitude on humans. It can start to occur above 8,000 feet, but usually doesn't have an effect on people until 10,000 feet or higher. It generally presents itself as a collection of nonspecific symptoms resembling a case of flu, carbon monoxide poisoning, or even a hangover. It is hard to determine who will be affected by altitude sickness, since it has no little or no relationship to one's physical level of fitness.

The causes of altitude sickness are not fully understood. The available amount of oxygen necessary to sustain mental and physical alertness decreases above 10,000 feet. Dehydration, due to the higher rate of water vapor lost from the lungs at higher altitudes, may also contribute to the symptoms of altitude sickness. The rate of ascent, the altitude attained, the amount of physical activity at high altitude, as well as individual susceptibility, are all contributing factors to the onset and severity of high-altitude illness.

In most cases, the symptoms of altitude sickness are temporary and usually abate as altitude acclimatization occurs. Exertion aggravates the symptoms. Headaches are the primary symptom used to diagnose altitude sickness, although a headache is also a common symptom of dehydration. A headache occurring at an altitude above 8,000 feet, combined with any one or more of the following symptoms can indicate altitude sickness: lack of appetite, nausea, or vomiting, fatigue, weakness, dizziness, light-headedness, insomnia, pins and needles, shortness of breath upon exertion, nosebleed, persistent rapid pulse, drowsiness, general malaise, swelling of hands, feet, and face, and diarrhea. [I had many of these symptoms every day throughout the trek.]

"Altitude Sickness." Wikipedia, The Free Encyclopedia. Wikimedia Foundation, Inc. 21 Feb 2013. Print. 26 Feb 2013. http://creativecommons.org/licenses/by-sa/3.0/

Symptoms which may indicate life-threatening altitude sickness include pulmonary edema (fluid in the lungs), persistent dry cough, fever, shortness of breath even when resting, cerebral edema also (swelling of the brain), a headache that does not respond to analgesics, an unsteady gait, gradual loss of consciousness, and retinal hemorrhage. [I had a few of these symptoms as well.]

Acute mountain sickness can progress to high-altitude pulmonary edema, otherwise known as HAPE, or high altitude cerebral edema, otherwise known as HACE. HAPE occurs in about 2 percent of those who are adjusting to altitudes of about 10,000 feet or more. It can progress rapidly and is often fatal. HACE is also a life-threatening condition that can lead to coma or death. It occurs in about 1 percent of people adjusting to altitudes above 9,000 feet. Immediately descending to lower altitudes may save those afflicted with HAPE and HACE.

Ascending slowly is the absolute best way to avoid altitude sickness. This is the reason why we had "rest days" built into our itinerary. Once above 10,000 feet or so, most climbers and high-altitude trekkers take the "climb-high, sleep-low" approach. For very high-altitude climbers, a typical acclimatization regime might be to stay a few days at a base camp, climb up slowly to a higher camp, and then return to base camp. A subsequent climb to the higher camp then includes an overnight stay. This process is then repeated a few times, each time extending the time spent at higher altitudes to let the body adjust to the oxygen level there and encouraging the production of additional red blood cells. Once the climber has acclimatized to a given altitude, the process is repeated, with camps placed at progressively higher elevations. The general rule of thumb is to not ascend more than 1,000 feet per day to sleep, but even less the higher you go in extreme altitude. This process should never be rushed and is generally why climbers need to spend weeks acclimatizing themselves before attempting to climb any of the highest peaks, like Everest or K2.

Even though I was familiar with most of this information, having read it many times, I felt more freaked out than ever before, while sitting there and listening to it all. None of this information did much to boost my morale. It was important, however, for Lorraine to educate us on the dangers of AMS, and she accomplished her goal. This trek is not supposed to be easy. Lorraine's job is to protect us and she takes it seriously. It is her intention to scare us, just enough to get our attention. Many people have died here as a result of altitude sickness, although most of those fatalities have occurred higher up, toward the summit of Everest. Regardless, she needed us to be aware and to be cognizant of potential symptoms.

At this very moment, the temperature is nineteen degrees. I feel the chill penetrating my skin and cutting into my bones. I left my tent an hour ago, around 9:00 P.M., to go to the outhouse. I urinated for two continuous minutes, the result of all of the water I drank yesterday. It was the longest piss I ever took in my life. I must have looked like one of those garden statues, standing in one position with a constant stream of pee coming out of me, like a fountain.

I attempted to hold my breath in order to not breathe in the stench of excrement everywhere, but it wasn't easy. At this altitude, my heart beats at a much higher rate than usual, from the slightest physical efforts, and my asthma is restricting my lung capacity. I kept my nose hidden under my jacket to mask the awful odor. It was so cold my fingers became numb. When I went into the teashop to warm them up, Lorraine was there. I told her I couldn't feel my fingers and she told me I should keep my hands close to my genitals to warm them up. I responded by telling her I was taking a whiz and that's how they became numb in the first place. She laughed. I'm glad I amused her.

I'm in my tent right now, which I refer to as the icebox, bundled up tightly. I'm thankful the day is finally coming to an end, although the evenings here offer a different challenge from hiking during the day. I'm not sure which is ultimately going to be more difficult; the physical hiking during the day while being sick or trying to stay warm once we arrive at our camp site.

It's hard to accept the reality that for the next ten days, my body is going to be under constant duress from the frigid cold every single second that I'm not trekking or in my sleeping bag, but there's nothing I can do about it.

What the Travel Brochure should have said:

Day 6: NAMCHE BAZAAR • 11,300 feet

We continue trekking along the banks of the Dudh Kosi, crossing the majestic river time and time again on terrifying suspension bridges that will make you cringe with fear. If you have the nerve to walk across them, as terrifying as they appear, you'll be rewarded by having to cross yet another. You'll probably be working physically harder than you have in a long time, if ever. If you're sick, you're screwed. What were you expecting, a walk in the park? Look at the bright side though. Today's hike will be easier than every other day from here on. So enjoy it if you can. Relax and have a cold piece of toast with peanut butter and jam, or some hot oatmeal and broth, along with some Fanta orange soda. Get used to it, since it's basically what you'll be eating every day, along with your energy bars, for the next eleven days, with few exceptions.

CHAPTER THREE: SELF-DOUBT

4

MURPHY'S LAW

"We either make ourselves miserable, or we make ourselves strong. The amount of work is the same."

-Carlos Castaneda

11-13-04

TRAVEL BROCHURE DESCRIPTION:

Day 7: NAMCHE BAZAAR • 11,300 feet

Today is a rest and acclimatization day in Namche Bazaar. Namche is a colorful village, with many wonderful and interesting shops, vendors, fabulous food and stunning views of the surrounding mountains. An early hike above town, before the clouds move in, will reward climbers with a spectacular Himalayan sunrise and views of Mt. Everest, Lhotse (the 4th highest peak in the world), and the beautiful Ama Dablam.

Trekking Company Menu:

Wakeup tea / Coffee / Hot Chocolates

B/F:
Muslee, Butter toast, Onion Omlet
Tea / Coffee / Hot Chocolate

Lunch:
Cheese Sandwich, Mustard Salad, Luncheon Meat, Bag Beans
Tea / Coffee / Hot Chocolate

Refreshment
Tea / Coffee / Chocolates with Biscuits and snacks

Dinner:
Chessus Macaroni, Mess Potato, Beans Boil, Bring al Tempura, Cocktail fruits
Tea / Coffee / Chocolates

THE TREK

8:15 P.M., still in town of Namche Bazaar

Today was referred to as a rest day, but I didn't rest at all. I wasn't interested in spending the day worrying about how I was feeling and pondering whether I could make it to the summit. So I decided I needed to keep busy. I joined most of the group, to go hiking for a few hours.

Just as we were leaving town, we passed a school, where some of the children were practicing a dance routine outside. There were about eighteen kids between the ages of five and ten years old. They were all adorable and I immediately thought of my girls back home and how much I missed them. Half of the children were singing while the other half danced. All of the girls had long, straight dark hair and wore solid, bright red shirts over multi-patterned, red and blue long dresses. Incongruously, they all wore bright red lipstick. The boys were dressed in long white pants and long white shirts with brown vests and danced along with the girls. The children were apparently preparing for a performance, just like each of my girls have on numerous occasions in their schools, 7,500 miles away.

As we continued on, I joined up with Lorraine and welcomed the chance to talk with her. She told me she is an avid rock and mountain climber and has been guiding treks in the Himalayas for a few years. She loves doing it, but said the pay isn't great and is therefore thinking about going into business for herself. We got into a long discussion about business in general and taking risks in life. I told her that if she is courageous enough to trek here and face the horrendous conditions without hesitation, then starting a business should be a no-brainer for her. I told her a bit about myself, about having worked in sales and marketing for many years, and having recently focused on Internet advertising. We talked for a while about marketing and how she could acquire customers and probably spent a good hour or so discussing different ideas for growing her future business.

We hiked up a ridge where we had clear views of the summits of Mt. Everest (29,035 feet) and Lhotse (27,940 feet) and full views of Ama Dablam (22,349 feet.) (My kids love the name Ama Dablam, because they think it sounds like "I'm a dumb blonde," and they always laugh uproariously whenever I mention it.) Ama Dablam translates as "mother's necklace" or "mother's mountain." It is an incredibly beautiful, picturesque mountain. To many, the side ridges look like a mother's arms raised high, in order to welcome and protect her child. The name is adopted from one of the glaciers on the mountain, which looks like a *dablam*, a sacred ornament pendant worn by women in the Sherpa community in Nepal.

The summits of Everest in the upper left and Lhotse in the center, both behind a mountain range, and Ama Dablam in the upper right.

Me, with Ama Dablam in the background.

We are still a significant distance from Everest and need to trek many more miles to Gorak Shep, the camp site at 17,000 feet nearest Base Camp and Kala Patthar. During the hike today, I learned some facts about Everest that I hadn't known. Most interesting was that Everest, along with much of the Himalayas, is still growing. I always had the height of Everest implanted in my brain at 29,028 feet, since it has been published as such for many years, but it's actually slightly taller (according to the U.S. National Geographic Society.) Depending on the source, Everest is currently classified as being anywhere from 29,015 feet to 29,035 feet high. (China classifies it as the former number since they don't include the snowcap.)

The Himalayas began to form approximately seventy million years ago and are among the youngest mountain ranges on the planet. They were formed as a result of a collision between the Indo-Australian Plate and the Eurasian Plate. They are still growing a few millimeters per year. Everest will continue to grow taller for millions of years, before it eventually begins to shrink under its own weight.

After we hiked as a group, I went on another hike by myself. I was trying to acclimate to the altitude as much as possible. I was glad I had it in me to explore further, but some of the bravado was just a cover for not wanting to be miserably cold back at the campsite. I ascended almost one thousand feet above Namche Bazaar. It didn't seem as though I had climbed as far as I did, since I surprisingly felt fine doing it, but I was wearing an altimeter watch which indicated I was above 12,000 feet.

There wasn't a single cloud in the sky on the way up. The sun was shining intensely and the heat made me feel like an egg in a frying pan. Even though the temperature gauge on my watch only read thirty-five degrees Fahrenheit in the mid-day sun, I was working up a major sweat from struggling so hard. My body was soaking wet underneath all of my layers.

When I reached the high point of my hike, there were wonderful views of the mountains and of the whole town of Namche Bazaar. It was unexpectedly, a colorful town with a kaleidoscope of colors. When I hiked into town yesterday afternoon, in a heavy mist and complete cloud coverage, everything seemed gray. But today, from up high, it was a stunning sight with blue, green and red rooftops dotting the landscape. There was vegetation immediately surrounding the outskirts of town and there were tall mountains enveloping everything, with bright, snow-capped peaks. The tents at our campsite appeared as tiny yellow specks. I took in the view for a while, but thought I should get going.

View of Namche Bazaar from above the town.

Within a few minutes of heading back down into town, the clouds blew in and the temperature started to drop precipitously. Moments earlier, I had been bathed in sweat from the hard, hot climb, but suddenly I was freezing cold. And to make matters worse, I wasn't producing any body heat as I descended. Why couldn't it have been cloudy and cold an hour earlier as I was ascending and burning energy, and have been sunny and warm when I was descending and not utilizing any real effort? It was just my luck.

I recalled a couple of memorable hiking trips where I encountered similar examples of Murphy's Law. The first was during a hike up Longs Peak, a mountain over 14,000 feet in Colorado. A few minutes after reaching the summit, immediately after noon, I began to descend. I was well aware that the weather is highly unpredictable in the early afternoon in the Rockies. Out of nowhere, a spectacularly violent electrical storm blew in. The dense, almost-pitch-black clouds were in spitting distance above my head, turning day into night instantaneously. The continuous laser-like lightning strikes were turning the mid-day darkness into fleeting strobe-lit scenes. They were visually beautiful, yet mindfully terrifying and destructive. The continuous thunder booms, occurring in unison with the lightning due to their deadly proximity, were so loud and explosive they shook the stone earth beneath me. I was certain I was going to die.

There are specific rules one should follow during lightning storms, such as crouching low on the tips of your toes and, of course, ensuring you're not carrying anything which can possibly conduct electricity. Unfortunately, during a raging electrical storm when your life is at risk, you tend to forget, or, ignore, all of the rules. I ran for my life. I eventually made it back down to my campsite…and thanked God I was still alive.

And then there was the trip to the Grand Canyon with my friend Mark. As we were driving to the Canyon after midnight, one of the tires on our rental car blew out. This caused us to be late and we missed the opportunity to get a pass for camping at Phantom Ranch, the camp site at the bottom of the Grand Canyon and the only lodging facility below the Grand Canyon rim. Then, when hiking into the canyon later that day, I almost stepped on a rattlesnake. Within seconds of joking how unlucky we were, the largest hailstorm we ever experienced began pounding us. We used our backpacks to cover our heads as we searched for refuge from the barrage of golf ball-sized frozen projectiles, which struck every part of our unprotected bodies. Since there was no place to take shelter in sight, we decided the only option was to run back up the trail as fast as possible. After a few minutes, the hail turned into a torrential downpour, soaking us completely. The water was rushing down the trail with tremendous force, cascading over our boots and way above our ankles. We made it back to the rim and reached a small lodge along the West Rim Road, with a roaring fire burning in a large, stone fireplace. We took off our drenched hiking boots and put them near the fireplace to dry. We had a bite to eat. An hour later, we finished eating and grabbed our boots, which were fiery hot, and carried them with us back to the car, walking barefoot. We checked into the hotel and had a great night's sleep and departed early for another hike, toward the Bright Angel trailhead. The six-mile, downhill hike to Plateau Point was astonishing, and we experienced the beauty of the canyon in all its glory. I figured our bad luck was behind us.

After enjoying the views and having our lunch, we started ascending back up toward the trailhead. Within seconds, I starting feeling some discomfort in the back of the heel of my boot and thought I had a rock in it. I stopped to check, but there wasn't anything there. It turned out that the rubber heel on the back of my hiking boot had melted in the fireplace while drying out the prior day. I hadn't noticed it on the hike into the canyon earlier, because my foot shifted toward the front of the hiking boot while descending. However, now that we had started ascending up the canyon, my foot had shifted to the back of the boot, applying tremendous pressure against the deformed heel and causing a massive blister. I ended up taking off my hiking boots and walked, without shoes, up the Grand Canyon for the next five miles – slowly and painfully – while attempting to avoid both the rocks in the trail and the mule manure, which was everywhere. It took me almost six hours, under a wickedly searing

100-degree sun, to get back up to the top of the trail. Murphy's Law…on steroids.

I returned back to my tent in Namche Bazaar and changed into warm, dry clothes. Afterward, I walked through town and purchased an amazingly delicious pizza from the Namche Pizza House and Sandwich Bar. Once again, Nepalese pizza proved to be as good as any New York-style pizza I have ever had. I wasn't sure if it only seemed this way since I hadn't eaten much in the past week, but I didn't care since it hit the spot. While there, I ran into Teddy and Mitch, who were just finishing their pizza. They informed me that they were heading to a shower facility.

Although I hadn't planned to take a shower, I decided I should do the same. I assumed it would be the last time I'd be showering for at least a week. I went back to my tent and grabbed some soap and shampoo and then tracked down the place.

The facility looked as if it had never been cleaned. There were muddy bars of soap, discarded wrappers, empty tubes of shampoo, and, dirt and grime everywhere. I gathered that almost every trekker passing through Namche frequented this filthy facility, whether on their way up or on their way down the mountain, along with many of the town's residents. I hesitated to take a shower, since the conditions were so unsanitary. However, I had discovered by then that everyone else in the group had showered, so I felt obligated to do so as well.

Afterward, I decided to do a little shopping in Namche. It is a tiny village, and the only really active, commercial town to speak of above Lukla, with a few hundred small buildings – mostly clothing and souvenir shops, teashops, lodges and homes – in the middle of the mountains. Namche is the primary trading area for the entire Khumbu Valley. There's a post office, a police station, a bank, and many Internet cafes. There are merchants offering all sorts of jewelry, arts and crafts, tchotchkes, and of course, hiking gear. Anything new with a well-known brand name on it is likely to be counterfeit gear.

There are, however, some legitimately branded, second-hand items for sale. These are items that belonged to descending trekkers who donated them to their Sherpas and porters. Those same Sherpas and porters then immediately sell the gear in town for whatever price they can get for it. And the prices are dirt cheap. You could buy either a brand new, but most likely counterfeit Northface down jacket for $50 or a legitimate, but dirty, second-hand one for the same price.

Some of the impoverished locals selling the used gear live in small tents and sell their wares right from their tent door – in essence, a permanent flea market – at 11,300 feet above sea level. This large tag-sale-like gathering takes place right at the entrance to Namche Bazaar as you arrive from Phadking.

The more established merchants, located in buildings and stalls, are situated slightly higher up the hillside. There are probably a dozen pathways loaded with vendors and there are a few eating establishments nestled in between them. I purchased a hat made of yak hair with soft fleece on the inside for $3.50.

I put this hat on as soon as I bought it and didn't take it off the entire trek, except when I was in the shower. [I even continued to wear it for a few weeks after I returned home, which my wife found very odd.]

I also purchased a fleece neck warmer for $3.00, a pair of brand new windproof gloves for $4.00 and a fleece sleeping bag liner for $6.00. Although not on our original "tour company shopping list," a friend had mentioned to me that a sleeping bag liner was a life saver at high altitudes. [She was right.]

There are close to four hundred households in Namche with almost two thousand residents. It is disturbing for a Westerner to see how people live here, especially those working at the flea market, yet for all I know they may consider their lives completely fulfilling – maybe even more so than mine. From the little I have been able to converse with the porters and Sherpas, they've made it clear to me that the people here are content.

I know people don't need material things to be happy in life. I certainly live a life full of creature comforts, but if I didn't have them, I'd survive. I might sulk a bit, but I'd get over it. A few years ago, I was driving by a church and it had a sign in front that read "The only things you need in life are not things." I try to remind myself of this on a regular basis.

Many of the Nepalese people who live here in the Himalayas came from Tibet hundreds of years ago to escape persecution in China. Much of the goods sold here are carried over those same mountains. Life is hardscrabble in this harsh landscape. But people still manage to enjoy themselves. As a matter of fact, it's 8:30 P.M. right now and I hear people singing, as I did last night as well – late into the evening. I guess when there's not much else to do in Namche Bazaar late at night, you hang with your friends and family and sing.

For dinner, the chef whipped up some spaghetti and yak meatballs. I ate some spaghetti, but passed on the meatballs. Most people wolfed them down and some even had seconds. They loved them and, of course, started cracking jokes about them. Someone started calling them yak balls and I started laughing to myself, remembering the *Saturday Night Live* Schweddy Balls skit with Alec Baldwin. It was one of the funniest skits I ever saw in my life. I brought it up to the group and we ended up talking about a bunch of other *Saturday Night Live* skits.

I still have not had any meat on this trek yet. The sight of it nauseates me in an instant. I also won't eat dessert here because the only thing they serve is canned fruit and I won't eat canned fruit.

When I was a little kid, my mom kept a pantry full of canned fruit in the house. My dad ate an entire can of fruit every day; peaches, cherries or pears, all in heavy syrup. Although I ate it as a kid and enjoyed it because it was loaded with sugar, I haven't eaten canned fruit in decades.

What the Travel Brochure should have said:

Day 7: NAMCHE BAZAAR • 11,300 feet

You're thankful that today is a rest and acclimatization day in Namche Bazaar. You're going to be sore from the strenuous hike yesterday. At this point, you're probably not feeling very well. You are beginning to develop bad headaches from the altitude. Your stomach isn't feeling much better. Don't sweat it; just accept it. You're going to be dealing with these problems, and much more, for the balance of the trip. You're also probably starting to freeze your ass off, but do keep in mind that it's not nearly as cold today as it will be over the next few days. So chill. Get it? Catch some rays. Take a dirty shower. Have an amazing pizza. Enjoy it since it will be your only good meal for the next week. If you have the energy, an early hike above town will reward climbers with spectacular views of Mt. Everest, Lhotse and the beautiful Ama Dablam. You should check it out because if you decide to abandon the climb over the next few days, this will be the only chance to see the mountain you came to see – the spectacular Mt. Everest. Don't worry, things could be worse. Actually, they will be, so hold on tight.

5

FAITH

"Life without faith in something is too narrow a space in which to live."

-George Lancaster Spalding

11-14-04

TRAVEL BROCHURE DESCRIPTION:

Day 8: TENGBOCHE • 12,687 feet

The trek continues along the rushing glacial waters of the Dudh Kosi with magnificent views of the mountains. We will spend the night next to the Tengboche monastery, the spiritual center of Khumbu region. Inside the monastery are incredibly ornate wall hangings, a 20-foot sculpture of Buddha, and the musical instruments and robes of the Lamas. If our group is lucky, we will see the Lama perform a ceremony and hear the mystical chanting and music.

Trekking Company Menu:

Wakeup tea / Coffee / Hot Chocolates

B/F:
Corn-flakes, Bread toast, Cheese Omelet
Tea / Coffee / Chocolates

Lunch:
Juice, Cheese Chapati, Chips, Salad, Boil Cauliflowers,
Tea / Coffee / Chocolates with Biscuits and snacks

Dinner:
Spagetti with pasta Sausage, Potato Rubi, Green vegetables, Fried Yak Meat

Desert
Tea / Coffee / Chocolate

3:30 P.M., town of Tengboche

Today was another really tough day. It started off poorly, since once again I couldn't sleep. There was a pack of stray dogs near our campsite, barking and brawling all night long. Every time a couple of them barked, all the other mongrels throughout the entire town of Namche Bazaar joined in harmony. The noise drove me crazy. I started to take it personally, thinking it was meant specifically for me. "Did I do something wrong to deserve this? Is God out to get me?" As hard as I tried to ignore the dogs, including using earplugs, nothing worked. They finally started to settle down by 3 A.M. My body is in such dire need of sleep that it is affecting my ability to function.

Every time I tell myself it can't get any worse, it does.

At 5 A.M., the cooks started preparing breakfast, making a terrible racket. They clearly couldn't care whom they might wake up in the process – although this assumes someone had actually managed to fall asleep. They rattled the pots and pans so loudly that the dogs near our campground started barking again, in turn causing all of Namche's dogs to join in unison. It was a chorus of canines – the head cook conducting his crew with their instrumental kitchenware and the "bow-wow chorale" howling their songs in harmony. The noise echoed through the entire town of Namche Bazaar, as if we were in a large amphitheater.

The porters came to our tents to wake us up at 6:30 A.M., as though anyone could possibly still be asleep. (I'm not sure if I fell asleep at all last night.) I went through the morning ritual at a much slower pace, since my brain was lacking both shuteye and the necessary nutrients to allow it to function. It is the fourth day of the trek and I've hardly eaten anything nutritious. It's not just because the food is so bad. I simply don't have a desire to eat anything. Any food that is put in front of me nauseates me. I've started forcing myself to eat more energy bars, but it's not easy. Although I usually enjoy them, they become rock-hard here in the cold weather. It's like biting into a brick, and then chewing leather. It's even harder to swallow them, since they are stone dry and rip at my sore throat. My Gu has fortunately come in handy, since it glides smoothly down my throat. It's too bad I didn't bring more. I typically don't think about using Gu as a replacement for a meal, but I should have.

We started trekking at 8:30 A.M. toward the Tengboche Monastery. We had to descend from Namche in order to cross the river on another suspension bridge. We went down a steep, narrow trail, descending approximately five hundred feet, around huge boulders and through heavy brush, eventually reaching the river. As we walked across the bridge, the whooshing roar of the rapids was a calming sound in sharp contrast with the continuous barks and growls of the previous night. The sound of a rushing river is, to me, one of nature's greatest compositions – music to my ears. The fresh, clean smell of the river, blowing in the breeze created by the rapids, was intoxicating. I was feeling optimistic being in this magnificent place – of course, while descending.

We have crossed the Dudh Kosi River many times the past few days and will continue to do so, following it much of the way up the mountain. The river flows from the summit of Mount Everest – and we are basically headed in that exact direction. Unfortunately, and as usual, the earlier descent necessitated a significant climb back up, and then some, to the tune of two thousand feet, in order to reach Tengboche.

We had not even gained the original five hundred feet we descended earlier, before I became exhausted, yet I needed to keep pushing forward. Fortunately, the sun was shining the entire morning during the early portion of the ascent, and it gave my body the strength to push forward. As bad as I felt, the slight warmth – spreading through the cold morning air – comforted me. The bright sunlight brought every tree and leaf into crisp focus and gave me a more optimistic perspective regarding my efforts. It was reassuring for me to know that as rundown as I was feeling, and being at the mercy of the mountain, there was still a resplendent source of energy helping get me through the day. It compensated for the lack of fuel in my body and helped sustain me along the path, acting as a powerful counterbalance to my despair.

We hiked along the river, through a predominantly wooded area, for much of the morning. Fortunately, the man-made trail created just enough of a clearing along the path to allow a few slivers of the sun to break through the swaying leaves. The tranquilizing beams flickered in my eyes as I took each step. My mind wandered constantly, with dozens of different thoughts, but the consoling rays prevented me from dwelling too long on any one subject. I was in a meditative state, which was a good thing, since it took my mind off of the trekking.

We stopped briefly for a horrible lunch consisting of a quesadilla-like item which was stone-cold, and bland cauliflower – not that cauliflower ever has much flavor. Of course, I barely ate anything. In place of it, I had an energy bar.

Unfortunately, the clouds rolled in immediately after lunch and the temperature quickly dropped. With the sun gone and my energy depleted, the rest of the hiking day became a colossal challenge. I quickly became severely downhearted and was in a terrible funk. I somehow managed to stay on the path through nothing less than sheer will, step after step after step. I just kept staring at the rocks and stones the entire time, hypnotized by the thousands of them, in every shape, size and shade of white and gray. Other than the rocks on the trail, I can't recall much of the last hour or two of hiking.

Toward the end of the hike we were walking in the clouds, and my head was, figuratively, in them as well. It was if I were dreaming, or worse, as if I had died and was floating overhead. The more we hiked, the more I entered a hypnotic state. My body and my mind again went onto autopilot, just as it had the other day on my way up to Namche Bazaar, when I was similarly exhausted.

Despite being barely conscious, I managed to turn into the very last switchback, after walking up scores of them in the heavily wooded area. I took the few remaining steps up the same sort of dirt path I had been on all day, and dragged myself over a two-foot ledge to the monastery. My heart felt like it was beating out of my chest, as I was huffing, puffing, and gasping for air.

At once, the forest disappeared in a puff of smoke, or rather, a dense mist. It seemed as though I had landed at heaven's door. I knew I wasn't dead, but for all intents and purposes, I could have been.

After having climbed through steep hills, heavy brush, and tall trees for hours, I was suddenly confronted with a huge, flat field on which sat the monastery. If I didn't know where I had been headed when I started out this morning, I would have thought for sure it was all a dream, or a mirage, but the fact that I did know helped bring me back to reality. Miraculously, I had reached my destination, and more important, I had conquered another day.

Although I'm not really sure how I pulled it off, I made it to Tengboche by 3:00 P.M. It is freakishly cold right now as I write this. Our duffel bags and tents have not yet arrived. The porters got off to a late start today. Of course, Jack and Ian arrived earlier and were waiting for the rest of us, looking well-rested. I don't understand how they made it up here so quickly. They must be unbelievably fit. It bothered me. Is it just youth? Was I as fit as they were when I was younger? Or, am I just really out of shape after all of these years? I know that I haven't kept up my exercise regimens like I used to, but I thought I had done enough to prepare for this trek. I must be in worse shape than I thought.

The entire team arrived at various points throughout the afternoon. I certainly wasn't one of the first to arrive, but I wasn't the last either. Even though it wasn't a race, I didn't want to establish a reputation for myself of being the last to arrive each day. It was only by pure chance that Randy and Robin moved more slowly than I did, at least today. Time will tell.

There are just a few buildings here in Tengboche. Instead of waiting for the porters outside in the cold, we just walked into the Tengboche Bakery. Beside the monastery, a bakery was not the first thing I expected to find here. Although the pastry choices here are sparse, and none offering a shred of nutrition, the place is a godsend. I am hungry and luckily, there are certainly enough items of interest to choose from in order to satisfy my hunger. Every pastry looked like a typical croissant one would expect to find in any American bakery. The bigger question I had prior to buying any of them was trying to figure out what was stuffed inside of them. I asked the baker to provide me with one plain pastry and one stuffed with cheese. I made it very clear that I didn't want a meat-filled one, assuming it would be yak meat.

Although the bakery is slightly heated, I am shivering. My clothes that are in contact with my skin are soaking wet from the taxing climb. I was cold and miserable while trekking all afternoon, and mentally unprepared for what I went through, hour-by-hour. I'm sitting inside, trembling, while slowly eating my pastries and writing. It is evident that every person on our trek, except (possibly) the fast guys and the guides, are having second thoughts. Although nobody has openly said it, I'm confident everyone is thinking the same thing -- "What sane person would ever want to pay for the privilege of dealing with this fucking nightmare? What was I thinking?" I can't wait to crawl into my warm sleeping bag and pass out.

5:00 P.M.

The town of Tengboche ("boche" meaning town or place) is no larger than a few thousand square yards or so. Lorraine informed us that "Teng" translates into "foot" and "Ding" means hand. Tengboche is the location where Lama Sangwa Dorje, the founder of Tengboche, left a footprint in a stone (hence, "foot place.") Dingboche, where we are heading tomorrow, accordingly means "hand place." Normally, I would be interested in some further explanation of these names, but feeling as I do, I have no energy, nor desire, to ask additional questions. It is a sad state of affairs when I can't muster the energy to ask a question about a place I am visiting for the first – and last – time.

Outside of a few outlying buildings and the monastery, this place is desolate. There are thick, ominous clouds overhead. If you were dropped into the town for an afternoon, you'd be amazed by the flawless architecture of the monastery in the middle of the Himalayas. You'd be blown away by the surroundings – the snow capped peaks way out in the distance. However, if you're living, sleeping, and eating (or at least trying to do so) in these mountains for two continuous weeks, it's a very different and unpleasant experience. As hard as I'm working at it, I can't get myself to find any pleasure in the moment.

After an hour or so, while still waiting impatiently for our gear to arrive, we grudgingly agreed we should visit the monastery. We figured as long as we were here, we should take advantage of the opportunity. We knew we wouldn't have time to do it tomorrow since we will be leaving for Dingboche early in the morning. Although it was surely an incredible feat building the monastery at this altitude, none of us had enough energy to actually be excited about seeing it. We were physically wasted. Regardless, we decided to check it out.

Tengboche Monastery

The Tibetan Buddhist monastery was first built in 1916, but destroyed in an earthquake in 1934. It was rebuilt shortly thereafter and then destroyed again due to an electrical short-circuit causing a fire in 1989. It was once again rebuilt with international assistance, and is now the largest gompa in the Khumbu Valley.

The monastery was beautiful from the outside, but not any more so than many of the Asian places of worship I've had the good fortune to visit, and certainly not as architecturally impressive as the Tiger's Nest Monastery in Bhutan, which I have not (yet) visited. It was still quite impressive just the same. We went inside, but we were not allowed to take pictures, so I'll do my best to describe it. The first thing we noticed when we walked in was a giant golden Buddha, probably ten or more feet tall, wearing red lipstick and wrapped in what looked like a very colorful blanket or sari. There are various sized, but much smaller, Buddhas, surrounding the larger one.

The main prayer room, no larger than a typical public school classroom, is decorated in vivid colors and there are beautiful, colorful paintings and Buddha statues everywhere. The room contains intricate carvings in the walls, ceilings, and support columns. We were informed that many of the old scriptures, murals, and wood carvings, among other precious items, were lost in the fire fifteen years ago. The new carvings are painted in pastels and had a calming effect on me. I could also have been feeling calmer because the monastery was heated and I was exhausted. Whichever it was, it provided me some mild comfort. I so wanted to enjoy being there and appreciate the beauty of this revered sanctuary. I know how important this place is to so many people, but all of my energy was drained from my body.

When I was leaving the monastery, I spotted the friendly, beautiful Donna – and it was fate – yet again. Or maybe Buddha had something to do with it, since I said a little prayer inside the monastery. For the record, I didn't pray for Donna. I simply prayed for the strength to get me through the next ten days.

Donna looked wonderful. Seeing her familiar, cheerful, smiling face brought some additional warmth to my soul. She obviously was handling herself just fine. We hugged, our bodies briefly touching, and exchanged some pleasantries. She told me she was excited to be heading toward Ama Dablam and attempting to summit. She asked me how I was doing. I told her I had had a couple of rough days and the cold weather was really getting to me. She responded warmly, providing some consolation, by simply telling me I will get through it and it is all par for the course for anyone trekking in high altitude in the Himalayas – especially first timers. Her words were reassuring. Her confidence, and her beauty, flicked the switch on my internal thermostat and had the effect of raising my body temperature a couple of degrees. Although I very well could have been imagining it, her super-friendly attitude made me feel she was coming on to me. When I said goodbye to her, she actually looked a bit disappointed, as if she had been expecting me to say something else to her. As I walked away, she shouted, "Good luck." I turned around, smiled, and said the same in return, as she entered the monastery.

As I walked away, I felt good – momentarily. I hadn't had a woman show a strong attraction to me in many years. I wasn't sure if she was actually coming on to me, or if I was imagining it, but I let my ego enjoy the moment.

By the time we came out of the monastery, our tents had finally arrived and were quickly set up. As I write this at this moment, I'm thinking how fortunate I am to have booked a single tent on this trek, which enables me to place my duffel bag and gear right next to me in the tent. I can pack and unpack everything without too much difficulty. Most of the other trekkers have tent-mates. Even though doubling up provides some companionship, I can't imagine it's at all comfortable. Anyone in a double tent has to not only fit two people, but also two massive duffel bags, into a tent the exact same size as mine. I guess it's not bad if you're with a partner and want to create some body warmth, but in any other instance it has to be uncomfortably cramped. In addition, feeling as bad as I've been feeling on the trip, the last thing I would want is to share my misery with a complete stranger.

Even though I have a single tent, it is still a hassle every time I attempt to leave my tent for any reason, whether to go to the outhouse or the mess tent, since I always leave my hiking shoes outside of my tent. I don't want to drag any mud, human excrement, or yak dung all over the inside of my tent floor. My tent is my home and I make every attempt to keep the inside of it sanitary. In order to minimize my visits to the outhouse as we have ascended higher and as it has become much colder each night, I've been using a large plastic bottle for peeing. It is very clearly labeled, "Pee Bottle," for obvious reasons. Using the bottle has enabled me to avoid countless trips to the outhouse in freezing temperatures in the middle of the night. I also avoid the need to put on my hiking boots every couple of hours, and most important, I decrease the likelihood of stepping or slipping in feces, tripping over a rock, or getting injured some other way.

My pee bottle is one of the most critical items I brought with me on this trek. It isn't easy using it since my tent is only a few feet tall at its highest point. I can't stand up, so I need to be on my knees. I also need to be extremely careful unscrewing and screwing the bottle once I've used it the first time each evening, in order to ensure my urine doesn't spill all over my sleeping bag or my gear. This is easier said than done in the middle of the night on a slightly sloped, rocky ground. It has taken some very deliberate, careful movements in order not to mess up. Regardless, I'm certainly willing to go through the hassle in order to avoid the outhouse as much as possible, especially as the temperature continues to drop each evening. Again, I'm lucky to have a single tent, since I don't think I would be able to take advantage of the pee bottle if I had a tent mate. It would be challenging with a tent mate because of space limitation, and undoubtedly inhibiting with someone I don't know well.

This is the first day of many where we will not be eating our dinner in a tea shop, even though there are a couple of them here.

There are not many individuals who would decide to make a livelihood running a tea shop this far up the mountain, but there are a few – some very ambitious, crazy, or possibly, desperate people. Regardless, we'll be eating in the mess tent tonight. I am actually sitting in it right now, having some decaf tea while I write.

The weather continues to be frigid. It is highly unusual for mid-November. It's difficult to convey how much the weather is affecting me. It is undeniably uncomfortable being ice cold while waiting around an hour or two for dinner.

Back in Connecticut, I'm used to the temperature in my home always being a comfortable seventy degrees or so. Here, it is twenty-eight degrees Fahrenheit at the moment, late in the afternoon, and it will get much colder as the evening progresses. There's no escape from it. Even worse, it will be much colder as we ascend. Knowing what the conditions are going to be like for the next ten days is painful to contemplate. I can't even imagine how miserable it will be trying to sit through dinner tonight in a tent while we are all freezing our asses off. I certainly will have no desire to hang out here afterwards, and will therefore just dive into my sleeping bag immediately after dinner.

Luckily, we did receive some relatively good news. We were informed we will be getting a heater for the mess tent in a couple of days – although not soon enough. Lorraine and the Sherpas agree we can't eat in the mess tent under these unusually frigid conditions. The bad news, however, is that in order to get it here, one of the porters will need to go back down to Namche Bazaar to get it. We all thought this was absurd, but the sirdar, our lead Sherpa, didn't think anything of it. He said the porters go up and down these hills and valleys all of the time. It's second nature for them to trek up and down a few thousand feet per day. He said it was like any one of us going up and down a few flights of stairs in our home. (He did a great job of making me feel even more inferior than I've been feeling.)

For a porter, or a Sherpa for that matter, what they do every day is not just a job for them. Rather, it is a part of their life and something they completely take to heart. They are decent, caring, and considerate human beings who would sacrifice their lives for their clients if it came down to it. They are the firemen, policemen, and EMTs from back home, wrapped up into one.

8:30 P.M.

I'm finally starting to get into a routine here. It's not an enjoyable one, but it's a routine just the same. After hiking all day, I go back to my tent for a few minutes in the late afternoon and try to relax and write in my journal. (This is assuming the tents are set up and our gear has arrived, unlike today.) I'll then change out of my sweaty, smelly clothes. I particularly can't wait to remove my underwear after a day of hiking. One thing I really detest is wearing moist, smelly, sweat-soaked underwear. I always like to have a fresh dry pair on. Can you blame me? It's the little things in life that make a difference. I brought along a fresh pair for every single day of the trek. The trekking company had recommended bringing along only four pair of underwear, but I thought that was preposterous. We have no ability to clean our underwear and no place to dry them, so I'm certainly not going to wear the same pair of filthy underwear for two or more days at a time. So instead, I keep a plastic bag of clean underwear and another clearly-marked bag of soiled, sweaty underwear. I marked the soiled bag "BIOHAZARD."

After I put on the clean underwear, I put on my evening attire. Generally, this translates into four layers on my upper body, including long johns, non-cotton t-shirts, long-sleeve fleece shirts, and a down vest. I wear a down jacket on top of all those layers, and will actually sleep in it if I am very cold. On my lower body, I wear long johns, fleece pants, and cashmere socks. And I typically use sneakers in the evening, in order to give my feet a rest from the heavy hiking boots.

After I change into warm clothes, I head to the teashop (or, as of today, the mess tent.) The cooking staff serves hot tea, coffee, cookies, and crackers. Occasionally, they serve a bowl of peanuts or some other snacks, but I won't go near anything that is shared – meaning anything where people have to stick their hands in a bowl. Everyone's hands are dirty from hiking all day. Even worse, some people come straight from the outhouse and dig right into the peanut bowl. I have no idea if they clean their hands or not, but there's no doubt in my mind that some of them do not. I'm certainly not willing to take any risks. It's also widely known that the locals here wipe themselves with their bare, left hand, after they defecate. They do not use toilet paper – just their left hand and water! Toilet paper is considered unsanitary! This fact is quite fresh in my mind each time a "community" bowl of snacks is passed around.

They just served some packaged salami to the table, so I may cut myself a few pieces to get some protein, before everyone starts handling it.

During tea, some of us play cards and others just hang out and talk about the events of the day. The conversation isn't very dynamic, since we're all exhausted. You'd think we were all dying. We have already answered the basic questions we had for each other the first couple of days, such as: Are you married? Do you have kids? Where do you live? What do you do for a living? So, most of the conversation has focused each afternoon on the hiking we had completed earlier in the day, and as important, what was coming up the following day. We each quietly hope that we will hear something soothing to our ears, such as "Tomorrow is an easy hike." But it's always more of the same from Lorraine; "we hike down to the river in the morning and then hike back up two or three times the distance." We do realize this is what we came for, to climb a mountain, but we silently wish and pray that we won't have to descend again. We are like little kids knowing our parents are going to deliver bad news because we are misbehaving, but foolishly thinking we'll get lucky and be spared.

One other topic that has been constantly discussed, or rather, made fun of, is Bollywood. When we were in Kathmandu, the television stations were airing Bollywood movies. Some of the guys thought those shows were hilarious, although I never really caught on to the humor. I'm not sure if it's because I don't feel well or it was just plain silly, or both. Regardless, they would discuss these movies it as if it was the only worthwhile topic. Every conversation, no matter how important or insignificant, somehow ended up with Bollywood playing a part of it. For the most part, I just listened and tried to find the humor in the conversation, which wasn't easy.

Other than cards and small talk, there isn't much else to do in the evening. Sure, you could explore a little bit if you really wanted to be adventurous, but it would be pretty stupid. It gets dark early. If you fall and hurt yourself, you're screwed. Besides, we are all too worn out to do anything except attempt to stay warm, settle back, and unwind. A few people try to take a nap, but I have no desire to do so, since I figure it would throw my sleep routine even more out of whack.

After tea, some of the team members go back to the tent to change into their evening attire. Since I do this prior to having tea, I stay in the mess tent and continue to talk with a few others who do the same. Unfortunately, the longer I stay in the mess tent, the more the temperature drops. It's quite noticeable, and disheartening. I get colder and colder as the evening progresses, and basically shiver the entire time until I'm back in my sleeping bag. Prior to the start of dinner, typically around 6:00 P.M., we step outside the tent, hit the outhouse, if necessary, and then wait in line to wash our hands.

We are not allowed back in the mess tent until we wash and scrub our hands. The staff pours a bit of hot water on our hands and gives us a bar of anti-bacterial soap, which is supposed to be white, but is actually black from all of our filthy hands. I also carry a bottle of anti-bacterial soap with me. After we all wash our hands, I then use my own soap to do a second scrubbing. And I also use it after relieving myself each time. It certainly hasn't helped me avoid getting sick up until now, but it provides me with a certain peace of mind just the same.

When I get back into my tent after dinner, I put "down booties" on my feet. I also keep two Nalgene bottles filled with boiling hot water by my feet, which the kitchen staff fills up just before I hit the sack. Everyone in the group does this as well. The water is always ice-cold by the morning. (I then use those same bottles of water as two of my three sterilized drinking bottles for the day.) And last, with all of my layers on, I slip into my fleece sleeping bag liner, which is inside my goose down sleeping bag – a bag that is rated to zero degrees Fahrenheit.

I'm hoping I can sleep tonight because tomorrow will be our longest hike thus far – almost eight miles. As usual, we descend during the early part of the day and then ascend later in the day. During this trek, we'll be hiking approximately thirty-five miles each way. It isn't too far in terms of actual distance, for me anyway, but when it's complicated by hills, valleys, altitude and all of the health problems and sanitary conditions, it's completely different from any trekking I've done in the U.S.

Someone told me tonight I should take some Diamox and it would help me sleep and adjust to the altitude change. So I'm trying it, even though it expired two years ago. I purchased it in September 2001, when I originally planned to go on this trek. I'm therefore not sure if it will actually work. Diamox is a diuretic and is supposed to help accelerate acclimatization. There is a negative side effect to taking Diamox. When a person takes it, or the generic equivalent, it causes frequent urination. More than you could ever imagine!

What the Travel Brochure should have said:

Day 8: TENGBOCHE • 12,687 feet

Having fun yet? Your punishing trek continues along the rushing glacial waters of the Dudh Kosi with magnificent views of the mountains, but you most certainly won't be able to enjoy them. Unless you are a triathlete, you will have a difficult time with the climb today. Yet, with determination and perseverance, you may just surprise yourself. Although the monastery is a sight to be seen, your poor health will prevent you from appreciating it. You will have views of Everest and other mountains from the camp site, if you're willing to leave the comfort and warmth of the mess tent or your sleeping bag long enough to take a look. If you do, bundle up. It's nippy out there.

A porter carrying tables and chairs up the mountain for the mess tent.

CHAPTER FIVE: FAITH

6

DARKNESS

"A journey is a fragment of hell."

-Bruce Chatwin

11-15-04

TRAVEL BROCHURE DESCRIPTION:

Day 9: DINGBOCHE • 14,250 feet

From Tengboche the trail drops to Debuche, crosses another exciting suspension bridge on the Imja Khola, and climbs to Pangboche amongst thousands of mani stones – stones and rocks inscribed with the mantra Om mani padme hum. Our uphill trek continues, taking us to the quaint traditional Sherpa village of Dingboche with its exquisite views of Lhotse, Island Peak, and Ama Dablam.

Trekking Company Menu:

Wakeup tea / Coffee / Hot Chocolates

B/F:
Porridge, Fried eggs, Pan Cake, Tea / Coffee / Chocolates

Lunch:
Juice, Tuna Sandwich, Cucumber Salad, Potato fried, Beans Boil, Tea / Coffee / Chocolate

Refreshment
Tea / Coffee / Chocolates with Biscuits and snacks

Dinner:
Rice Pullao, Meat Gravy, Boil Vegetables, mixed Salad, Desert Tea / Coffee / Chocolates

5:00 A.M., still in town of Tengboche

I just awoke from the craziest dream ever. I have no idea if it was related to the Diamox I took last night, or if it was something else that caused it, but it was wild. I hit the sack around 9:00 P.M. last night. As usual I tossed and turned for a couple of hours. Sometime shortly thereafter, I heard a voice. "David? David?" the female voice said in a soft whisper. I didn't respond and a few seconds later I heard the voice again. "David, are you in there?" this time slightly louder. I finally responded, "Yeah, who is it?" half dazed. I could see the beam of a flashlight moving around outside of my tent. A second later I heard the sound of a zipper opening on my tarp, the outer layer of vinyl material used to protect the tent and hiking boots from the rain, snow and wind. Then, a moment later, the tent zipper started opening. Half asleep and still confused, I wiped my eyes as the person started to enter my tent. I grabbed my flashlight and shone it in the face of the intruder, her head sticking through the unzipped tent flap. It was Donna.

"Donna, what's going on? What are you doing here?" I wasn't thinking very clearly at the moment. She responded, still whispering "I came to warm you up. Is that okay?" With the flashlight beam still on her face, Donna covered her eyes to prevent being blinded. I could see dense, steamy hot water vapors shooting out from her mouth as she spoke. It was nineteen degrees inside my tent. I was sitting up now, bewildered, still inside of my sleeping bag except for my head sticking out and my arm holding the flashlight. I pointed the beam of light straight up to the top of the tent, so as not to blind Donna. My brain was trying to do its best to register what was happening. There were a few seconds of silence, while Donna continued kneeling half outside of the flap of the tent, while the upper half of her body was inside and waiting for an answer from me. She repeated, "David, is it okay if I come in?"

Against my better judgment, and with an overwhelming amount of guilt, I decided not to insult her and make her go back to her tent. "I don't know...come in and close the zipper or we'll both freeze to death." Before she could move another inch, I realized her shoes might be dirty. "Take off your shoes!" Even in the midst of this craziness, I was still thinking about keeping my tent clean.

She was wearing slippers. She removed them immediately and entered the tent. She proceeded to close the zippers on the tarp and then on the flap of the tent. I could immediately smell the sweet, flowery perfume on her body. It was the same scent she had worn on the plane and it immediately brought back the memory of our first encounter. The sweet, strong aroma awakened me. She looked beautiful. She had obviously freshened up before arriving, unlike me – looking disheveled and having to pull out my night-guard retainer from my mouth, which I use to keep myself from grinding my teeth while I sleep.

I was starting to get aroused. She proceeded to tell me she hoped I didn't mind her intruding on me, but I seemed so dejected earlier today when she saw me and she just wanted to provide me with some companionship. I told her it was really very kind, but I didn't think it was a great idea, considering I'm married. She responded by saying it would be harmless and I wouldn't even have to mention it to anyone, adding, "Nothing will happen." I thought to myself, "Sure, that's what all of my divorced friends said at one point as well."

Although I knew it was an awful decision, I relented and shook my head up and down slightly, softly whispering, "Okay." As much as I would love to deny it, my decision seemed to be a conscious one...or at least semi-conscious. She gave me a smile, took her jacket off and unzipped the rest of my sleeping bag.

"What do you think are you doing?" I asked myself. But I didn't stop her. She asked me to get out of the sleeping bag so we could use it as a blanket to cover both of us. She began to cuddle up next to me, both of us lying on our left sides, with Donna behind me. It was a bit cumbersome getting comfortable and ensuring we could both fit on top of the narrow mattress pad beneath us. She pulled the sleeping bag on top of us and wrapped her arms around me and I instantly felt warm again. We were spooning tightly. I hate to admit, but it felt amazing. It immediately reminded me of Faith and me spooning in our bed back home. We used to love to spoon, especially when sharing a full size bed which we did for a few years after first being married. It was not a good thought, since I was very keenly aware of how spooning oftentimes leads to something more than just cuddling. The guilt level was rising – fast.

After a half hour or so, we were in the exact same positions. I was still lying on my left side and she was still behind me. Every part of the front of her body firmly was pressed into every part of the back of mine. I was just beginning to think nothing would happen after all, since I certainly wasn't going to be the one to initiate any foreplay. Maybe she was serious when she said it would be harmless. A few moments later, however, I felt her hand move ever so slightly. Maybe she is just making her arm more comfortable? After a couple of seconds, I realized it wasn't harmless, and a rush of adrenaline, or maybe it was testosterone, overcame me and sent a powerful rush to my head, and elsewhere.

Her hand was moving slowly off the center of my chest and drifting down, ever so subtly, over my stomach and then further south. It didn't take a genius to know what was happening. I was yelling to myself not to let her do it, but a part of me was lobbying for her to continue and simply suggesting, "Let's see where it goes dude – chill out." Within a few seconds, her hand was over my crotch, on top of my clothing, and she gently started massaging me, first slowly and then more firmly. I was already fully aroused of course, from having a beautiful woman, doused in perfume, spooning with me. I could feel my heart beating through my groin area.

I don't know what I was thinking, but I couldn't ask her to stop. Or rather, I didn't want to ask. It felt too good. For the entire past week, I had been at a very low point in my life, and now she was making me feel wonderful. She was taking me from the lowest of lows to the highest of highs in record time, without the use of an illegal substance.

I have never had an affair. I have been loyal to Faith for fourteen years of marriage, and then some, and this was the first time in sixteen years that I had been with another woman. I realized at that moment there was almost no turning back. I was about to board a flight to hedonism, yet I was acknowledging to myself that the only ticket available for purchase immediately afterward would be a ticket to hell. I was well aware that hell hath no fury like a woman scorned. Faith had mentioned those exact words to me when we first got married, yet I was seconds away from reaching the point of no return.

At that very same moment, as I recalled Faith's words, I remembered something Donna had told me a week ago. She had wanted to have a child, even though she didn't have a partner in crime. It immediately dawned on me that this was all (very possibly) part of a larger scheme to accomplish her goal and have the child.

My head was filled with fear and panic. I already had three wonderful daughters and had no further plans for more children in my life. I started thinking of my girls. How would they feel about this, when they eventually found out – which they would at some point? "Girls, guess what? You have another sibling."

I immediately started returning to my senses, although I'm sure some of my buddies would argue I completely lost it at that moment. As difficult as it was to do, I told her I was sorry, but I couldn't proceed any further. I asked her politely to go back to her tent. She started to do so by beginning to move off of me, but then quickly attempted to pull off my pants. Luckily for me, I was wearing a few layers, so it wasn't as easy as she thought it would be. If she had been successful getting her bare hands on my genitals, then all bets would have been off. Regardless, she kept pulling firmly. She wasn't taking "no" for an answer. She pleaded, "Come on David, I want you so badly. Live a little."

"Donna, you are beautiful and I am so turned on right now, but I can't do this. Please try to understand." I was struggling to hold onto my pants while she was fighting to pull them off. I grabbed my pants with a fast, strong tug and she lost her grip and fell backward into the corner of the tent. I fell back in the opposite direction and hit my head on my flashlight, and woke up from the sudden impact to my head.

I couldn't believe it. For a while, I wasn't even sure if what I had just experienced actually happened or not. It seemed so incredibly real. When I gained my composure, I realized it in fact had just been a dream, but almost as real as life. Just to be sure however, I pointed the flashlight all around the inside of the tent to make sure Donna wasn't there. There was no sign of her, nor was there any lingering scent of her perfume.

I had never had such a vivid dream in my life. Whether it was the Diamox, or being so overtired from not sleeping much the past week, I'm just glad it was a dream. I never would have been able to live with myself if it had actually happened. I love you Faith.

I'm going to try to go back to sleep for a couple of hours, since we don't have to start getting ready until 7:30 this morning.

4:00 P.M., Dingboche

Today's hike was unbelievably rough. I am very ill. I'll update you tomorrow.

What the Travel Brochure should have said:

Day 9: DINGBOCHE • 14,250 feet

There will be plenty of ups and downs, physical ones and emotional ones, more misery, and more grotesquely disgusting outhouses to visit. Basically more of the same shit! By this point, you're sick to your stomach and you're cursing yourself for coming here, and the fun hasn't even begun yet. All kidding aside, you're truly screwed the next few days — but don't give up. You came here for a reason.

Arriving into town of Dingboche.

7

RESUSCITATION

"They have seen but half the universe who never have been shown the house of pain."

-Ralph Waldo Emerson

11-16-04 Rest day

TRAVEL BROCHURE DESCRIPTION:

Day 10: DINGBOCHE • 14,250 feet

Our second and last rest day. There is the option of taking a light acclimatization hike up the valley for a wider variety of photos of the valley and mountains of the Khumbu region.

Trekking Company Menu:

Wakeup tea / Coffee / Hot Chocolates

B/F
Muslee, Butter toast, Vegetable Omlet
Tea / Coffee / Hot Chocolate

Lunch
Juice, Puri, Potato with Steam cheese, Sarden Fish, Salad
Tea, Coffee, Chocolate

Refreshment
Tea / Coffee / Chocolates with Biscuits and snacks

Dinner
Italian Spaghetti, Boil Cauliflower Tampur, Green Vegetables, Yak Tika

Desert
Tea / Coffee / Chocolates

7:00 A.M., town of Dingboche

T oday is a rest day. Thank God. The last twenty-four hours easily goes into the record books as the worst of my life.

I woke up in Tengboche yesterday morning, after the crazy Donna dream I had in the middle of the night, with a terribly upset stomach. Unfortunately, the previous evening, I ate some beef salami, which looked and smelled fine, even though it did nauseate me a tad while eating it. I thought it would be safe to eat, since it was pre-packaged, and believed it would be a good idea to have some protein. Maybe it was safe to eat, maybe it wasn't. Maybe it was the pastries from the Tengboche bakery. Who knows? Anything could have made me sick. There are dozens of possible causes, but it doesn't really matter at this point.

I had foolishly discontinued my Cipro dosage a couple of days ago when my stomach started to feel slightly better. As I've mentioned, my doctor had advised me in the strongest terms to not stay on Cipro for more than a couple of days, but I think I made a terrible mistake taking his advice.

The hike itself, to Dingboche, wasn't overly difficult, especially after having struggled so much the previous few days. Our expectation was that each consecutive day would be more and more demanding. Thankfully, this was not the case yesterday. We descended only slightly in the morning before we hiked a full eight miles of gradually increasing terrain. We gained almost 1,800 feet in altitude, but it was over a long, manageable stretch – not the very steep pitches we've been climbing thus far. I barely remember anything at all about the trail, the scenery, or anything else for that matter. For all I know, it's possible the hike was in fact very difficult, but I was so ill that my body overcompensated for it somehow. Or maybe I was so focused on how bad my stomach felt and how nauseated I was that I didn't think about the effort I was exerting.

My stomach felt worse and worse as we hiked throughout the morning. Around mid-morning, I started feeling light-headed and dizzy, and continued to feel this way throughout the balance of the day. I'm not sure if this was because of my bad stomach only, or if the altitude had something to do with it as well. I recall frequently waiting to use multiple outhouses along the trail, with numerous people from my group, along with others on the trail, waiting in line in front of me each time we stopped. Many of them were feeling equally awful. At one point, I had to go to the outhouse so badly that I thought of asking everyone in line in front of me if I could cut to the front of the pack, but I knew they were probably as sick as I was, so I did my best to take my mind off my stomach while "holding it in" and hoping, actually praying, not to have an accident.

I didn't eat anything for lunch yesterday, and I also hadn't eaten much for breakfast. This certainly didn't help with the lightheadedness since my body was operating on fumes, but I couldn't take a chance of eating something and feeling even worse – nor did I have an appetite to eat regardless. Immediately after the group stopped for a lunch break, and prior to starting out in the afternoon, I felt so ill that I had to ask one of the Sherpas to carry my backpack. Four other guys on the trek who were also ill had already given their packs to the Sherpas earlier in the morning. When I first witnessed this, I thought to myself, "Come on guys, your pack only weighs fifteen measly pounds. It can't be that bad?" Well, after feeling as sick as I did, I understood completely what they were going through. I just wanted to curl up in a hole, or close my eyes, click my heels three times while saying "there's no place like home," and end up back in Connecticut. Since neither of these options was possible, I gave my backpack to Dawa, a charming and fit Sherpa. I was so appreciative that I wanted to hug him to thank him, but I didn't have the energy to lift my arms, so I just said "thanks" in a pitifully weak voice.

Shedding the fifteen pounds from my back was like lifting the weight of the world off my shoulders. Instead of feeling like a frail, one-percent of my usual self, I now felt like two-percent. As bad as that sounds, it was still a hundred percent improvement. I was taking anything I could get.

I kept slogging along, without any awareness of my surroundings. Instead of the hypnotic state I had been in the past few days while I was hiking, I was now completely incoherent. Although the smart thing would have been to throw in the towel and ask Lorraine to provide me with a Sherpa to head back down to Lukla, I kept moving forward, like a zombie. I'm not sure if it was pride, determination, or stupidity, but in all probability, it was a combination of all three. I was cursing myself incessantly for coming here. I wanted to be home.

The afternoon was a complete blur, so I won't even attempt to describe it. The only thing I specifically remember was seeing the town of Dingboche in front of me as I came around a bend, and taking a picture. The only reason I took the picture was because I saw others doing the same and figured, robotically, that it was probably something I should be doing as well if everyone else was doing it.

To say I wasn't feeling well at dinner last night would be a major understatement. It wasn't enough that I still had a terrible cold, hacking cough, sore throat and an awful headache. I was freezing cold – trembling with what was possibly the start of hypothermia – and trying to understand how I had put myself in such a situation, knowingly, with no help nearby. I felt awful in every possible way. Even so, and as bad as my stomach felt, I thought it was absolutely necessary to get some food in my stomach. I believed I needed to eat. My body was desperate for some nourishment in order to attempt to heal it – or so I thought.

So, at dinner, I decided to have a steaming hot bowl of tomato soup. I figured a bowl of boiling soup couldn't be bad for me. I believed I'd feel better after eating it. It certainly tasted great, since I hadn't eaten much of anything in days. It also felt absolutely wonderful going down my wickedly sore throat, soothing the pain. I thought I had finally made the right decision and was glad to get something in my stomach that didn't nauseate me.

I returned to my tent to with the intention of going into hibernation in my warm cocoon, hoping I would sleep for a full day, since I knew I didn't have to hike the next day. I was truly grateful, feeling as sick as I felt, that I was being given a "get out of jail free" card by having a "rest day" today. Unfortunately, this feeling of gratitude was all-too-brief.

It was twenty-two degrees inside my tent. I was at 14,250 feet above sea level and I had a throbbing headache – most probably from the altitude – but no doubt further aggravated by numerous other issues. No matter what I did to try to assuage the pain in my head throughout the day, including taking multiple doses of aspirin and trying to stay hydrated by almost drowning myself with constant water intake, the headache not only persisted, but worsened. I was despondent.

Within minutes of getting into my sleeping bag, I felt my tent spinning. I closed my eyes to try to make it stop, to no avail. Seconds later, as I lay inside of my cocoon, my guts started churning. It seemed like a major battle between "good" and "evil" was brewing in my stomach. I knew this awful feeling quite well and I was terrified of what was about to occur. I've had this feeling a few times before in my life, but this time felt worse than ever – and this time, there was also no doctor or ambulance nearby to help me out. I was desperately hoping that "good" and "evil" would work out their issues and save their battle for another day. I was praying for a miracle, and asking God to intervene so I'd feel better instantaneously. Unfortunately, my prayers went unanswered. I was absolutely dreading my impending doom. Would it last for minutes or hours, or perhaps even days?

I started having debilitating stomach pains. This wasn't just my stomach churning. The pain was excruciating. It would have made me curl up in agony if I wasn't already curled up in a ball trying to comfort myself and get warm. I grudgingly acknowledged it was either food poisoning or a terrible bacterial infection. Aren't they basically the same anyway? The answer wasn't important. On the food poisoning scale of misery, with a

"1" indicating discomfort and a "10" indicating intense pain, mine was a catastrophic "50." I've had food poisoning before. And, it was agony. However, as bad as I felt then, I was fortunate to be staying in a warm hotel room, which had clean toilets, clean towels, and, most important, someone to comfort me.

I was in North Carolina on a business trip. Faith had accompanied me on the trip and joined me for the business dinner. I ended up eating some tainted pulled pork. I was awake all night with my head in the toilet. However, even in those darkest hours, my wife was at my side with a cold compress. She had a constant supply of clean towels to wipe my face. She rubbed my back. The bathroom was clean. It even had air freshener in it and smelled beautiful. Even though it was a terrible experience, to this day, I have more fond memories of it than painful ones. It's amazing how the human brain has the ability to block out the kind of pain I experienced that day, but still enables me to retain the positive experience of my wife comforting me.

Knowing I had no control over what was about to occur, I attempted to prepare myself, by getting my mind and body ready for the apocalypse. The Richter scale in my stomach was registering 10.0. "Come on David. Just deal with it. You'll get through it."

Faster than a speeding bullet, my stomach sent a cataclysmic message to my brain. Alert! Alert! S-O-S! Get your lazy ass out of this sleeping bag NOW or you will regret it for the rest of your life! Until that very moment, I had tried for as long as possible to "will" the pain and nausea away, without success.

I knew I couldn't hesitate, even for a nanosecond. I sprung out of my sleeping bag like a compressed, industrial-sized coil being released. I unzipped my tent in record time and threw on my boots, which were sitting outside of the tent flap, leaving my laces untied. It probably took me all of twenty seconds to do this, where it should have taken three or four minutes. (I was already wearing my layers and my jacket in my sleeping bag at this altitude. Thank goodness for this, since it would have been a horrific sight if I had to take the time to get dressed.)

I then made a mad dash for the outhouse. Not even ten yards into my sprint, I slipped on some ice and went flying into the air, doing a backward half-somersault and fell flat on my back. I was inches shy of my skull following through on the impact – but thankfully stopped short. It was a scene out of a cartoon, with the victim slipping on a banana peel and screaming "#%*(@#*!" The fifty-yard passage to the outhouse, to my huge dismay, had turned to ice from the trampled, wet mud earlier in the day – basically becoming an ice skating rink. It was a miracle I was able to hold in the contents of my insides.

I stood up as fast as possible, not thinking of the pain I should have been in from the fall, and continued toward my destination – slipping and sliding the entire way – while still doing my best to prevent myself from soiling my pants. I came incredibly close to slipping again, a few times, and had an image quickly enter my mind, of me falling, cracking my head open, and freezing to death in a pool of blood, vomit, and excrement.

I finally made it to the outhouse with no time to spare. The split second I opened the door, the stench hit my sense of smell like a brick. I'm not sure if it reeked worse than it had on any other night, or if I was just so terribly ill that it seemed so much more offensive. Whatever the reason, it was categorically and undeniably sickening. As hard as it may be to believe that my physical condition could have gotten any worse at that moment, it did, with lightning speed. The walls of the outhouse were gyrating like a centrifuge, with me being the axis, trying to balance myself and not fall flat on my face into any one of the dozens of piles of shit surrounding me. It was the worst case of vertigo I have ever had, yet I didn't have a moment to spare.

"Move, move, move!" Completely disoriented, with the world whirling around me, I forced myself into position as best I possibly could – while doing my darnedest to avoid the usual obstacles. I wouldn't have really cared if I happened to step in shit at that moment, since I had much more important things on my mind. While trying my damnedest to not breathe through my nose, and with my flashlight wedged between my biceps and my ribs, I pulled down the multiple layers of pants, long johns, and underwear in record time. I squatted down and almost simultaneously had an explosive volcanic eruption, with blistering hot molten excrement bursting out of me, searing my ass and destroying everything in its path.

For a brief moment, there was an amazing sense of relief. How I mustered up the strength to hold it in until that point is truly beyond me. I gave myself a quick mental pat on the back.

As much as I hoped I was going to feel better immediately after this tsunami, I didn't. I tried to quickly clean myself off, but due to the need to breathe – for obvious reasons – and since my heart was beating at a thousand miles an hour, I inhaled. B-I-G mistake! The atrocious smell set off a violent chain reaction, from my nose to my brain to my stomach. Instantly, the vertigo came rushing back again. I did an immediate about-face, bent over facing the exact same hole I had just crapped in, and vomited the acidic tomato soup I had eaten a couple of hours earlier, burning my throat.

As soon as I stopped vomiting, I tried my absolute hardest not to breathe. Yet as soon as I took a gasp for air, being unable to make my getaway quick enough, the fetid air of the outhouse forced me to gag and vomit some more. It was a vicious cycle, vomiting, breathing, vomiting some more, until I finally gained my composure a few minutes later, thinking I had nothing left inside of me to regurgitate.

I headed back to my tent like a wounded dog, thinking I could finally get some rest. Unfortunately, the torment didn't end. It continued for what seemed like an eternity. I ended up going back and forth to the outhouse a half-dozen more times, experiencing the exact same horrors. It was as if it were Groundhog Day, except instead of waking up in Punxsutawney, Pennsylvania, which would have been paradise, I was reliving an absolute nightmare. After each outhouse visit, I rushed back to my tent, took off my hiking boots, crawled into my sleeping bag and attempted to fall asleep. Actually, I prayed and asked God to allow me to fall asleep. Yet, as soon as I managed to get the slightest bit comfortable, the warning bell would go off in my head telling me to make a run for it again. And each time, I went through the same process, climbing out of my tent, putting on my boots, almost slipping on the ice, etc.

Every time this happened, I thought of the movie *The Karate Kid*, but instead of "wax on, wax off," it was "boots on, boots off," "tent open, tent closed," "pants down, pants up". Each time I entered the outhouse, I tried to prepare myself for the olfactory onslaught. Yet consistently, I failed. I was so paralyzed by my symptoms – dizziness, nausea, lightheadedness – I was unable to think clearly and protect myself from my own sense of smell. And then the vomiting would start again, and again, and again. Each time I returned to my tent, I prayed I had nothing left in me. Each time, until the very last, I was wrong.

Finally, after what I think was the seventh visit to the outhouse, my body sensed it was finally over. There wasn't a shred of anything left inside of me. My body had expunged every last ounce of anything that wasn't physically or organically attached to it. I paused for a moment, just a few feet away from the outhouse door, gasping for fresh air and breathed a long sigh of relief. As cold as the air was, I sucked it in with long deep breaths in order to clear my lungs, and psychologically take me to a better place.

I took a few more steps and then leaned against a wooden railing, to make sure I had regained my balance. I had been so dizzy for the past couple of hours, and I also barely had the energy to stand. While resting there for a few seconds, I started to slowly gain my equilibrium and clear my head, taking in the crisp, cold air. I was able to observe my surroundings, first the campground, then the teashop, and then the silhouettes of the imposing mountains encircling the entire town of Dingboche. As tranquil and still as it all seemed, it was especially moving to me to be experiencing an incredibly serene moment after the previous hours of horror.

I hadn't given any thought to the fact that even though it was the middle of the night, I was able to see everything around me. I wasn't even considering what was shedding this brilliant light on the entire town. I simply wasn't thinking. My eyes were working, but my brain was still in recovery mode.

As I shifted my eyes further north over the tall summits and on to the horizon, I was awe-struck. I looked up even higher into the night sky and was blown away by what I was seeing. All around me were hundreds of thousands of dazzling bright stars. The entire universe was glowing right in front of my sick eyes. At the current altitude, I was three miles high in the sky in thin air, in a place without a single particle of air pollution (except for the outhouse of course) and not a cloud in the sky blocking a single star.

There was only a slight crescent moon, enabling the stars to sparkle and glisten with an amazing intensity beyond anything I could have ever imagined, lighting up the entire town enough for me to see clearly. Never before had I had such a magical view of the night sky.

I pointed my flashlight at the ground to make sure it was clean and bare. I then crouched down on the ground and lay on my back. I turned off my flashlight, looked directly upward, and looked at the sky for what was probably five minutes. For the very first time on the trek, the cold weather felt invigorating as I viewed the sky in complete and utter amazement. I experienced the cosmic irony of its perfect beauty in contrast with what I had just lived through moments earlier — one of the ugliest, lowest points in my life.

As I took it all in, I felt I was being sent a message that everything was going to be okay, and that no matter how bad I felt, there was still a beautiful world for me to experience. I reminded myself that no higher power had anything to do with the awful experience I had just gone through. I chose to go on this trip. It was my doing. I put myself in this situation and now I had to do my best to live with it or simply turn around and go home. The choice was, is, and always will be, mine.

As I sit here and write this morning, I feel as if I'm on life support. I'm grateful the night is over, during which I barely slept a wink. It is an absolutely beautiful morning. The scenery here is magnificent, yet I feel too ill and weak to enjoy the views. I want to be able to feel like my usual self, to take pictures, and explore the surroundings. I want to be able to enjoy the Himalayas as I have dreamed of doing for so long.

Today is the last rest day. As much as I don't want to give up, there's absolutely no way I can continue if I'm still feeling like this tomorrow. I honestly don't know if I can take this punishment anymore. My body is so weak. My stomach is hollow. I must force myself to eat something today and I must hydrate.

I never thought I'd actually consider surrendering, but I might. Is it really worth it to continue? I don't want to contemplate this choice right now because if I try to think about it logically, there's no way I'll be able to justify going forward. Almost anybody with a half of a brain in my state of health would weigh the pros and cons of going higher and surely opt to wave the white flag. But I have never given up before on any challenge I've faced.

Later that day, around 1:15 P.M.

After some downtime this morning to recover, I'm feeling slightly more like my usual sick self – not the extremely ill person from yesterday and last night. I'm so grateful for the rest day today. There's no way I would have been able to gather enough energy to get back on the trail this morning if we had to keep going.

The town of Dingboche, at 14,250 feet, is pretty large in terms of area, possibly even larger than Namche Bazaar if I had to guess. However, the population is probably a fraction of one percent of Namche, if that much. There are a handful of buildings here, besides the few tea shops scattered throughout the town. What the town has are majestic mountains in every direction. There isn't any snow on the mountains immediately surrounding the town, but I can see the glaciers blanketing the higher peaks off in the distance. I am longing to feel good, so I can really enjoy being in this setting.

There are a few teashops here in Dingboche, so I will be able to get my daily supply of Fanta Orange soda. I have consumed more orange soda over the past few days than I have in my entire life. Soda never tasted so good to me. I'm not sure what it is exactly that makes me want to drink so much of it. It could be the sugar, which is providing me some much-needed calories, or the carbonation or both. Regardless, for me it's better than water. It's surprisingly difficult to drink plain water in extremely large quantities for two weeks. I just can't seem to get enough of it down my throat to meet the five-quart requirement suggested by Lorraine. So I compensate by drinking orange soda.

Our campground is on the property of a teashop. The owners provide, for a fee, an inside-dining area, where I am at this very moment. It's not a big room, but it can fit everyone in our group comfortably. There's no décor at all. It's just a room with a few wooden tables and chairs, wood walls, and a cast-iron stove. Most of the teashops and tea lodges are warmed by these small stoves, which are fueled not by wood, but by yak dung (yak poop.) There aren't any wood logs anywhere near here, of course. Trees don't grow at this altitude. And there are restrictions on logging in the Himalayas, in any case.

So somehow, many moons ago, someone figured out that dried yak dung burns well.

The yak dung is collected and flattened into a giant patty the size of an Olympic discus. It is then dried in the sun by sticking it to the outside of the teashop walls. Mitch quipped that someone, long ago, must have said, "Let's just throw some shit against the wall and see what sticks."

The only problem is it stinks – not only when it is excreted by the yak of course, but even more after it dries and is made into fuel and subsequently burned. I'm not sure what it is about yak dung that makes it smell so much, but I'm sure there's a scientific explanation for it. (I discovered later it's the bacteria in the feces.) When it's burned, it creates a thick smoke that permeates the room, clogging my sinus passages and exacerbating my asthma. I can barely breathe right now. As if I didn't have enough problems, I'm going to have to breathe in yak dung if I want to keep warm.

An hour later

After a brief attempt to withstand the noxious odor from the yak dung in order to stay warm, I regretfully chose to go back into my cold tent. I figured my sleeping bag was a healthier alternative for me.

Our tents are currently set up on an open area campsite in front of a Nepalese family's property, almost dead center in the middle of Dingboche. The elderly husband and wife who run the place have a granddaughter. I'm guessing she is four years old. She may, in fact, be their daughter, but I have no idea because they don't speak any English. They may just look old, because of the hardships of life in Dingboche and the lack of dental or health care.

The little girl is absolutely adorable. A few of us were entertaining her by playing a combination of hide-and-seek and peek-a-boo. She was laughing hysterically – having a grand time with us. She was clearly enjoying all the attention she was receiving, which probably doesn't happen every day. She is filthy, and seemingly hasn't been bathed in days or weeks. Or maybe she is simply a typical kid who likes to play in the mud. I don't know. Her clothes appear to have never been washed, but I have no idea if that is true. She's just a kid doing anything her imagination enables her to do in order to entertain herself – but doing it while permanently living at 14,000 feet above sea level and breathing in yak dung fumes every day of her life.

I was hoping, for the little girl's sake, that she was happy every day and had parents who loved her and did everything they could for her. I wondered what was in store for her as she grows older. Would she get a good education? Would she end up becoming a porter or a farmer? Watching her made me to think of my girls. I thought of them constantly this morning.

The heater for the mess tent finally arrived yesterday. It's so big that I can't imagine how just one porter was able to go lug it all the way back up here from Namche Bazaar. It's over two feet high and a foot in length and width. It must weigh at least fifty pounds. And it needs liquid fuel, not yak dung, to operate, so they needed to get another porter to tag along from Namche to carry the fuel. Unfortunately, when it's operating, it emits an awful smelling, toxic smoke. So we had to leave it halfway out of the mess tent, which diminished the warming effect.

Unfortunately, after having the porters lug it all the way up here, we're not sure if we even want to use it now. Do we prefer to eat in an ice-cold mess tent or in a moderately cold mess tent while breathing in poisonous fumes? It doesn't matter to me since either way I lose. If we eat in the mess tent and don't use it, I freeze. If we do use it, I will have problems with my asthma. And if we eat in the teashop, I'll be breathing in yak fumes, it will stink and I will also have a problem with my asthma. There's no winning.

11:30 P.M., End of the "rest" day in Dingboche

As I've mentioned, I didn't bring much Cipro with me. My doctor only prescribed five tablets because he felt so strongly about my not abusing it, and I finished the dosage – long ago. So I asked Jay this afternoon if he had any to spare. He didn't hesitate, reaching into his pocket and pulling out a small bag full of the tablets.

Jay could easily pass for a local drug dealer, but he isn't. What he really is more than anything else is an explorer, travelling around the world. He has covered much of the globe already and has no plans to stop. Shockingly to me, he came to Nepal without a camera. He doesn't want to take one single picture. He simply wants to enjoy life every day, exploring the planet, without any permanent memories

Jay, who is probably ten years my senior, has deeply-tanned and weathered skin that looks like worn leather. He also sports a scruffy beard, long hair, has tattoos all over his arms, an earring and a brown cowboy hat. He wears sunglasses all day until dinnertime. I like him and am glad he is trafficking strong stuff, double the dosage of my prescription for each Cipro tablet. I figured he purchased them somewhere in Katmandu, or maybe Canada or Mexico, because he travels so much. I had no idea, but I didn't care at that moment. I just needed the Cipro. He reached into the bag and pulled out a bunch and gave them to me. I thought he would ask for some money, but he didn't.

Being cautious and based on my doctors' warning, I broke them all in half to lower the dosage. I took one of the halves immediately. I took another one a few minutes ago, and I'll stay on them until I'm positive my stomach is healed. It seems to have done the job, since I'm starting to feel better already. The fact that I also don't have any food left in my body certainly doesn't hurt.

Since we had plenty of time to kill today, I decided to take a shower this afternoon. It had been a few days since I last showered in Namche Bazaar. During that time, I had sweated profusely each day, vomited dozens of times, and crapped scores more, while simultaneously visiting the most bacteria-laden, germ-infested outhouses on the face of the planet. I thought a shower would be a good idea.

There is a public outdoor shower at one of the teashops up the hill. There were a half dozen trekkers waiting in line for it when I arrived, since it appeared to be the only commercial shower in town. The shower itself looked like something you would see in an old western movie. It was a stand-alone wooden shack, approximately four feet long by four feet wide and seven feet high. The ceiling was basically a flat board, which had a bucket with a hole in the center of the base, sitting on top. The bucket was fastened to the roof, and connected by a hose to a shower head on the inside of the shower.

I stood in line for about fifteen minutes, in the cold weather. Fortunately, the sun was shining brightly. Even though the temperature was below freezing, I felt comfortable. When it was finally my turn, I took off my jacket and multiple layers of shirts and set them aside on a bench, leaving just my pants and underwear on while still standing outside of the shower, in front of everyone else who had gotten in line behind me. The shower was much too small to hold all of my clothes inside and not get them wet.

I stepped inside. There were no hooks on the inside. It had one very narrow shelf at my chest level, about five inches wide, large enough to barely hold a small towel and some clean underwear. I cracked the shower door open slightly and tossed my pants out on a dry area of the ground. I needed to keep the towel and underwear inside the shower. If I left them outside, I would have turned into an ice sculpture as soon as I opened the shower door, after being soaking wet. This would not have been a pretty site for the spectators still waiting in line for the shower. I would have immediately transformed into a very skinny, sickly looking ice-sculpture.

I was praying my towel and underwear wouldn't fall on the floor and get soaking wet and filthy from the muddy ground. The floor of the shower was bare earth, so the water from the shower and the constant flow of foot traffic from all of the trekkers turned it into sludge. I fortunately wore flip-flops into the shower, which the trekking company wisely suggested bringing along. It would have been very risky taking the shower barefoot, for so many different, yet obvious reasons.

So there I stood, stark naked and shivering in this small shack. The teashop owner had boiled a pot of water and poured it in the plastic bucket on top of the shower once I entered. When I was ready, meaning once I got the nerve, I pulled the latch and the water started flowing rapidly out of the shower head. If I had delayed doing this at all, the water would have cooled down quickly. I don't think I ever appreciated, until that very moment, boiling hot water hitting my face and dripping down my body. It was absolutely exhilarating – unlike any shower I had ever taken. The scourges of the past few days, along with the resulting sweat, vomit, bacteria, and general filth, were washing away and soaking into the muddy ground.

I tried to relish the moment, closing my eyes and remembering, for a few short seconds, being back home and taking a hot shower. I went to a safer place, ever so briefly – but then reality hit. I had no idea when the hot water was going to stop flowing. In all probability, it was going to be very soon. I tried to wash myself as fast as humanly possible. I needed to make sure the soap was off my body, so I moved liked a bat out of hell. Once the water stopped flowing, after forty-five seconds or so, I quickly began to morph into an ice cube.

I dried myself off in record time, while painstakingly ensuring my towel never touched the muddy floor. Then I did the same thing even more carefully while putting on my underwear. I obviously needed to remove the flip flops to put on my underwear, which required a graceful balancing act – delicately standing on one leg and then the other and putting my feet through the holes without touching the underwear with my still muddy feet. It was an acrobatic feat, performed while feeling dizzy with hunger and oxygen deprivation.

Unfortunately, and to my chagrin, I really didn't feel much better after the shower. Sure, I was clean, which was a good thing, but my insides were still a mess. My head was still pounding. I was lightheaded from not eating, still coughing constantly, and with a raw, runny, painful nose from my cold. The continuous cough aggravated my constant headache, as if someone was constantly throwing jabs at my brain.

At dinner, I was still nauseated, but I knew I had to eat something if I was going to hike another day. So I ended up eating some plain pasta. No sauce, no butter, nothing. Miraculously, I kept it down the rest of the evening. This was a major accomplishment considering what I went through yesterday. The Cipro was working.

The running joke amongst everyone in our group with intestinal problems, which is most everyone, is that if you have the confidence to fart, then you're probably feeling better. One of the guys told us that he tried to let one rip last night, thinking he only had gas and he ended up defecating inside his sleeping bag.

Luckily for him, it wasn't a mother lode and even more luckily, he was wearing his long johns, so it didn't leak into his sleeping bag. And, most fortunately, he had the opportunity to shower today. The truly sad thing, however, is I understood immediately how it happened. When you consider how terribly cold it is at night and also consider how most people would do anything in order to stay inside of their fabulously warm sleeping bag if they were ill, it doesn't take a rocket scientist to realize the dangers of not moving quickly, or the danger of incorrectly assuming you have gas, when it's actually something much worse. As difficult as it is both physically and mentally to abandon the comfort of your cocoon, and confront the bitter cold, the slightest hesitation in doing so can be disastrous.

I was speaking with Teddy earlier this evening. He summed up the trip so far in one word – "suffering." I told him a more appropriate word would be "torture." I suggested that, "Suffering is the result of being tortured on this trek."

While lying in my cocoon a few minutes ago, unable to sleep, and thinking about this entire trek, I thought of Francis. It helped me keep things in perspective.

Just one year prior to this trek, Faith and I had been volunteering for Make-A-Wish of Connecticut, the local Connecticut chapter of the national organization that grants wishes to children with life-threatening illnesses. We were asked to visit a ten-year-old boy named Francis, who had a rare form of bone cancer. We needed to work on granting his wish, as soon as possible. We visited the family and met with him. He was the cutest ten-year-old boy on the face of the planet, with dark hair and wire-rimmed glasses, who appeared wise beyond his years. I still remember his face vividly. He was ecstatic to meet us, knowing we were granting him a wish to do almost anything he desired. Yet still, he was in agonizing pain. I felt helpless, watching him as he suffered, but he was incredibly brave dealing with his illness, and his pain, while talking with us.

A few days later, Francis had the opportunity to experience part of his wish – a trip to Disney World – but had to be air-evacuated back home. He died soon thereafter. We were heartbroken. I had never known anyone who had died at such a young age. It was very difficult to come to terms with. One year after Francis passed away, his dad Carlos spoke at the one-year anniversary memorial. His speech moved me to tears, not just for the suffering he had been through, but also for the bravery he exhibited. He ended his speech by saying, "…we should just make the remaining years of our short life here on earth about caring and loving each other. There is no time for anything petty. We should reach out and help each other to the best of our abilities. We should make each day a celebration of what God has given us. In the end, what really matters is how we lived our life in relation to others."

So any time I speak of suffering, as I have consistently here, I fully understand that it's all relative. As rough as the trek was, I know I was getting off easy. And most important, I had voluntarily signed up for this "adventure."

I know that we each deal with pain and discomfort differently, and we each think it's the worst it can possibly be when we're physically and emotionally going through it. Having met Francis, I was well aware of this while dealing with my discomfort each day, and it is one of the reasons why I repeatedly did my best to suck it up. I can't even begin to imagine what Francis, or his family, went through each day knowing he was dying, or what his family has had to deal with every day after he passed away. Having three children myself, I can't think of anything comparable to the suffering caused by the loss of a child. I've tried to keep things in perspective ever since.

What the Travel Brochure should have said:

Day 10: DINGBOCHE • 14,250 feet. Today is the second and last rest day. You'll need it. There is the option of taking a light acclimatization hike up the valley for a wider variety of photos of the valley and mountains of the Khumbu region, but you won't do it. You'll need this day to fully recover and recharge your batteries or, should we say, your battered body. You haven't been eating. Chances are you've been hanging in the outhouse more than you prefer, and certainly more than you could have ever imagined. So try to relax and get healthy. Don't forget, you still have a few very hard days ahead of you and you need your strength.

A Nepalese girl who lived at the tea shop at 14,000 feet, playing "hide and seek."

8

TIMBER-R-R-R-R

"A journey indeed, is an emotional roller-coaster."

-Ana Monnar

11-17-04

TRAVEL BROCHURE DESCRIPTION:

Day 11: DZUGLA • 15,075 feet

From Dingboche the trail traverses through farmlands and meadows before continuing along the lateral moraine of the Khumbu Glacier. We will stop in Dzugla, giving our bodies plenty of time to rest and relax amidst the majestic mountains of Nepal.

Trekking Company Menu:

Wakeup tea / Coffee / Hot Chocolates

B/F:
Rice Porridge, chapati, Omlet
Tea / Coffee / Chocolates

Lunch:
Juice, Potato Paratha, Ham Meat, Green Salad, Boil Vegetables
Tea / Coffee / Chocolate

Refreshment
Tea / Coffee / Chocolates with Biscuits and snacks

Dinner:
Vegetable Roll, Tomato Sausage, Potato Thumb,
Cauliflowers fitter, Fruits
Tea / Coffee/ Chocolates

Early morning, still in Dingboche

I t's 6:30 A.M. and it is sixteen degrees inside my tent at this moment. Miraculously, and thankfully, my stomach is feeling much better this morning.

While lying awake half the night, and fortunately not having to go to the bathroom, I did a great deal of thinking. I was trying to determine if I should give up. I am not really sure if I will make it to the summit. Although I am feeling better, there is no guarantee that I will continue to feel this way for the next few days. We still have a very long way to go, but I can't give up – at least not yet. Since first becoming a teen, I have never given up on any challenge.

When I was younger, during my preadolescent years, I was a short, scrawny kid – the classic "97 pound weakling." I always thought of myself that way because of Charles Atlas, the bodybuilder, and his advertisements in the back of comic books. I loved reading comic books back then. And almost every single one of them in the early 70's had an advertisement from either the Johnson Smith Novelty Company, from where I would buy whoopee cushions and joy (hand) buzzers, among other things, or more pertinent to this story, the Charles Atlas Company. In his ads, Charles Atlas depicted a scrawny teen, the so-called "97 pound weakling," getting sand kicked in his face by a large muscleman, while the scrawny guy's girlfriend stands by, watching, and egging him on to do something about it. He goes home upset and is determined to get stronger, and get even. Sometime months later, after turning himself into a body-builder using the Charles Atlas system, the former weakling goes back to the beach and gets even with the big brute.

During those pre-teen years, a similar situation to what was depicted in those Charles Atlas advertisements happened to me – a couple of times, and weeks apart. The first time it happened, the instigator was one of two identical twin brothers (to this day, I have no idea which one.) Both brothers had reputations for being troublemakers, as did many other boys in my rough and tumble Brooklyn neighborhood, where being tough was much more respected than being intelligent, and wearing T-shirts with cigarette packs rolled into the sleeve was the fashion trend. One of the other tough boys, as an example, was nicknamed "Crazy Sal" and was rumored to have been in and out of reform school (as it was referred to at the time), and he also had a brother who was rumored to be in jail for murder. Whether the rumors were true or not didn't matter to young, impressionable kids. His reputation preceded him, and everyone steered clear of him.

Prior to my personal "sand-kicking" moment, I had always managed to do a great job of staying out of trouble, having quickly learned how to survive on the streets. When I was in elementary school, there was a fistfight every single day immediately after classes ended, and always on an empty parcel of grass the size of a large boxing ring, one block from school. The fights usually involved the same four or five boys, but with only two fighting at a time, just like a boxing match. The fight was sometimes a result of some silly disagreement that had occurred earlier that day – but oftentimes, the fight had to do with religious bias – probably more than I even realized as a young kid.

My school was made up primarily of Italians and Jews, but there was one boy, a Jehovah's Witness, who was targeted, or should I say bullied, frequently. He was a good kid and never created any real reason for someone to want to attack him, but the bullies did, constantly. He fortunately wasn't the smallest kid, so he always managed to hold his own, but still took a pounding. It was my first of many exposures to hatred and violence.

I had somehow learned how to co-exist with, and even befriend, the troublemakers in school. I never became *one of them*, but I managed to get them to like me in order to not get beaten up – sometimes through conversation, but more often through the use of candy. I was a candy fiend and always had sweets with me. I made no enemies and managed to stay out of trouble, until one day…

I was leaving my favorite candy store, having just purchased some candy and comic books, when one of the (identical twin) punks, and a friend of his, blocked the door from the opposite side. I asked him politely, yet loudly so he could hear me, to move. I repeated myself a few times, but he refused. After a few minutes, he finally relented, and proceeded to punch me in the face as soon as I exited the store, without provocation. I didn't fight back since he was much bigger than I was and, admittedly, would have easily beaten me to a pulp. And he also had his friend by his side.

Just a few weeks later, the punks' friend, who stood by and witnessed the first attack, saw me walking home from the same candy store. He and another friend grabbed me and held me, while he punched me in the stomach.

I realized at that moment that I needed to do something about it. I started lifting weights and began doing pull-ups and pushups. I may have even ordered the Charles Atlas booklet, but I can't recall, because since then I've ordered dozens of fitness related items through the mail (and through direct response television.) I became infatuated with guys like Bruce Lee and Chuck Norris. Bruce Lee died around the time this all happened, but I became a huge fan of all of his movies. I promised myself I would never, ever let those guys hit me again without making it hard on them. Fortunately, for whatever reasons, they never did approach me again. (I also grew ten inches taller over the next six years, which probably helped my cause.)

All through high school, I exercised religiously. I worked different jobs to support my purchases of weightlifting equipment, martial arts weapons – and photography equipment. The first job I ever had was working in a camera store, because I loved photography. Unfortunately, the owner of the camera store was the biggest bigot I've ever met, to this very day. He wouldn't help any customer who walked into the store if they weren't white – even if they had plenty of money to spend. This was just the tip of the iceberg. I witnessed a great deal of racism and hatred during my teen years in Brooklyn, and it bothered me tremendously.

In college, I took up Tae Kwon Do, while continuing to lift weights. After college, I returned home to Brooklyn and started working with my dad. I also started hiking. I would drive a couple of hours north of the city, initially taking on moderate hikes and ultimately, driving farther north, taking on much more difficult ones. I hated to run, so hiking on trails became my exercise of choice and, eventually, climbing moderately difficult mountains became my challenge of choice. Climbing served a few purposes. It was great from a cardio perspective. It gave me the chance to witness the natural beauty of the mountains, since there wasn't anything like it in Brooklyn. And it helped me challenge myself, knowing that the summit was always the clear goal. Prior to taking up climbing, I had been working out for years, but with no way of gauging success from my efforts, and no way of knowing if I had truly transformed myself.

I'm glad I was raised in Brooklyn. Overall, I had a wonderful childhood, with many positive memories, great friends and spectacular teachers who helped me learn and grow. And I believe I turned out (mostly) okay. I realize no place is perfect. My father-in-law has always said, "There's only one thing wrong with this world – the people." I've always loved that quote. I'm well aware that anything that happened in Brooklyn, because of some troubled individuals I came into contact with over the years, could have happened anywhere.

Sometimes life appears to be random. Whether it truly is or whether there is a greater force at work is determined individually by each one of us. Yet sometimes, shit happens. It could be a meaningless event that simply messes up your day, or it could be some horrible occurrence that can change your life forever, or anything in between. Once it has happened, it's up to each one of us to either do or not do something about it. For me, doing nothing has never been an option. I always see it as a reason to change things, hopefully for the better.

Of course it's easy for me to say this all now. But as a young child, when "shit happened" to me, it set me on a path that ended up impacting my life for a long time.

4:30 P.M., town of Dzugla

Today's hike was short and typically toilsome, yet uneventful. "Uneventful" is perfect, considering all I've been through lately. We left Dingboche at around 10:00 A.M. and arrived in Dzugla at 12:30 P.M. We trekked almost three miles. It was difficult, but strictly because of the altitude increase on the latter half of the ascent. Fortunately, it wasn't nearly as arduous as it was on some of the other days, even though we were trekking at the same steep pitch – mainly because we only had to do it for two and a half hours. Every other day has required at least five or six hours of strenuous trekking.

The first half hour was truly astonishing. There wasn't any trail at all. There was just a large expanse on the left shoulder of the mountain. It was relatively flat and as wide as two football fields. We actually could have thrown a football around if we had one, or even played Frisbee, which would have been more to my liking. Whether we would have had the energy to do so was beside the point. We hadn't seen or experienced anything like this thus far.

Within the first few minutes of starting out, on the outskirts of town, I walked across a small farm to take a picture. There were a few dozen homes and farms farther down the mountain, hugging the hillside, which we had not seen from the center of Dingboche. Way out in the distance, beyond the homes, there was complete cloud coverage extending deep into the bottom of the valley and rising slightly beyond our altitude of 14,000 feet. Above the horizon, on each side of the valley, there were tall peaks and clear blue skies. The sun had barely started rising beyond the horizon. It was reflecting off the clouds, causing them to glow with a brilliant luminescence. It reminded me of the final scene from the movie "Ghost," when Sam enters heaven, and more important, it was another sign for me – one of many the past few days, of how beautiful this world is and how I should persevere.

We continued up the wide open trail, if you could even call it that, which was basically packed earth with a few boulders spread throughout, with moss growing on top of most of them. The field was about a half-mile long – and quite wide at first – but narrowing rapidly the farther we advanced. Teddy walked right to the edge of the mountain, to take a look down into the valley. It appeared as if he was about to walk off of a precipice, which I guess he would have done if he had kept going. To the right of us was the mountain that we were working our way up, ever higher. Straight ahead and off to the left, we saw about a dozen tall peaks. A few of those peaks topped off at approximately the same general altitude that we were at, and we could see their summits in the distance. The rest of the peaks were anywhere from one thousand to a few thousand feet higher, with the tallest ones covered by glaciers. They were beautiful. The sky was a deep blue. It was a thrilling scene, and was made even more by the fact that the Cipro was keeping my stomach problems at bay. It enabled me to feel a slight sense of enjoyment, and to be a bit more optimistic about the upcoming summit attempt.

While stopping for a break today at a teashop, I needed to use the outhouse. The tiny shack was situated beyond the edge of a cliff and above a very steep drop. I was trying to figure out how they built it. It couldn't have been easy to construct the thing this high up and build it into the side of the mountain.

I hesitated before entering. I glanced at it from the sides, not getting too close to the edge. I saw the long support beams. There weren't nearly as many two-by-fours as I would have thought would have been necessary to support it, but I'm no carpenter, so what do I know? It looked solid enough, but my brain kept asking me "Do you really want to go in there?" Unfortunately, I had to go. The more I thought about it, the worse my stomach felt.

It's worth noting that this high up the mountain, it is getting more and more challenging to find a place to relieve oneself. At this altitude, outhouses are few and far between. If I have to urinate, it's easy. As a guy, I can relieve myself almost anywhere. It's much more difficult though if I want some privacy, in order to pull my pants fully down. I feel bad for the women, since they have to deal with this issue quite frequently throughout the hiking day. With all of the water we've been drinking, we have to constantly make pit stops. The guys relieve themselves almost anywhere when they have to urinate. Even though the women are perfectly willing to empty their bladder anywhere if absolutely necessary, they certainly prefer some privacy. Sometimes, in a wide-open hiking area above the tree line, there isn't any privacy to be had. In these cases, we do our best to help them out by looking the other way.

Thus, whenever there is an outhouse available, we all take advantage of it. So, I stood there deciding if I should put my fate in the Lord's hands and enter the "Cliff's Edge Outhouse." I figured hundreds of trekkers must have used it before me, so I went for it. I opened the door and slowly walked in, listening intently for any creaks with each step I took. I was silently praying the floor beneath me wouldn't cave in, causing me to roll hundreds of feet down the mountainside.

Upon entering, I immediately sensed something very strange however. It didn't stink. Well, it didn't stink nearly as much as the dozens of outhouses I had the unfortunate pleasure of frequenting thus far. I wondered why. I was confident they didn't have a janitor coming in and cleaning the thing out. I looked down through the hole in the bottom of the floor and immediately realized what was happening.

As usual, there was a hole in the floor for waste to pass through. However, since this outhouse was built into the side of the mountain, the feces from every trekker who utilized it didn't end up a few inches directly below the hole, accumulating with gallons of urine to the point where it became a giant vat of excrement brew. This outhouse was uniquely, and if I dare to say, refreshingly different. As I stood, or should I say squatted, over the hole, I looked through it straight down to the bottom. I saw one of the strangest sights I had ever seen. Situated many yards directly below me was an incredibly tall, inverted icicle of frozen solid shit. I did a double take, since I couldn't believe my eyes. I had seen just about everything on this trip — or at least every disgusting thing. This, however, won the prize. For the first time in a while, I had a good laugh — and was actually able to inhale in the process without gagging.

I was wondering how old the feces were at the base of this structure. I was also wondering what would happen once this pinnacle got so tall that it eventually reached the surface of the hole in the floor. Does someone come along with an ax every so often, position himself along the side of the base of this very tall, thin "pile of crap" and start chopping away? "Timber-r-r-r-r" I imagined someone saying, in Nepalese of course. This image will be implanted in my brain forever.

The town of Dzugla has two movie theatres, three nightclubs, a bowling alley, a sports complex, and a golf course. Just kidding. There's nothing here. Nada. I don't know if you can even call it a town. It has a couple of tiny shacks, each one acting as a home and teashop. Otherwise, it's desolate — just tons of boulders, of all shapes and sizes, spread out everywhere we walk or turn our heads. It's also very dusty here from the loose scree, the tiny, broken rock fragments found at the base of mountains or valley shoulders. The scree is easily tossed around by the blowing winds, further irritating my lungs and my asthma. Hovering almost right on top of us, just across an immensely deep valley, are fantastic, massive, serrated peaks, with their gray crags partially covered in white snow. It's an awesome sight. There are no distant landscapes to speak of, since these tall mountains fully surround us on all sides, essentially enclosing Dzugla. The entire small town is a moraine, a field, made up of boulders, gravel and clay, formed by the movement of glaciers down the mountainside over thousands of years. Glaciers, which are basically frozen rivers, form at the top of a mountain and move south ever so slowly, carving up everything in their path and ultimately forming the valleys in the mountains. As it snows, the glaciers get bigger. Eventually the bottoms of the glaciers get too heavy and separate from the newer, younger tops of the glacier. Any large opening in a glacier, looking like a huge crack from above, is called a crevasse and can be anywhere from a few feet deep to hundreds or even thousands of feet deep. Crevasses create huge and potentially death-dealing obstacles for climbers.

I'm still perplexed as to why Jack and Ian, the "fast guys," and also Jay, who has now joined them as part of their sprinting team, need to get up the mountain so quickly. They arrived way ahead of the rest of us, again. I have figured out one thing at least. They are heavy drinkers. San Miguel is the beer of choice here and it seems to me they are rushing up the mountain every day in order to have a few pints before the rest of the team arrives. When we arrived at the mess tent, the "fast guys" were all in a very good mood. It's hard to believe that the desire to have a few beers was enough of a motivation to spur them on, but I guess it's as good as anything else if that's their thing.

To tell you the truth, I am envious of them. When I was younger, I was extremely fit. I lived at the gym and exercised regularly. I probably could have kept up with them if I was fifteen years younger, or if I had simply taken better care of myself during that time. Instead, for the past decade and more, I chose a different path, working twelve or more hours per day since graduating from business school. It's amazing how an experience like this, as messed up as it is, can make me realize I need to better balance things in my life once I get back home. I can't change the past, but I can certainly change things going forward.

We had daal bhaat, basically Ramen noodles, for lunch today, the same noodles my daughter Reece loves and eats all of the time. I had never eaten them before today. I used to get upset with Faith for preparing them for her, since they're loaded with salt. I hate to admit it, but they tasted absolutely great, and the salt was probably just what I needed after losing so much of it over the past few days. I was also starving since I hadn't eaten much in days.

I am planning on hanging out in my tent this afternoon, just relaxing and reading a book until "tea time." I haven't had a long stretch at all to read. I've typically taken a half hour here or there whenever I could squeeze it in, which generally has been in the early mornings. In the evenings, I am way too cold and miserable, and I usually just try to force myself to sleep – unsuccessfully, of course. And in the afternoon, after hiking, I'm generally too busy changing into dry clothes, rearranging my backpack, moving gear around, etc.

At this very moment, Mitch is washing his hair with shampoo outside of his tent. He's giving everyone a good laugh, with a full head of white foam dripping down past his ears onto the ground, while fully clothed. Mitch has a fantastic sense of humor. He's been the class clown this entire trek. Others in the group are either hanging out outside and enjoying the "Mitch show" while trying to catch some rays to provide some warmth to their bodies, or exploring the limited grounds around the camp site. Mostly, people are just killing time. There's not much to do here or to look forward to – not dinner, not freezing your ass off in the mess tent, and certainly not the trekking we'll be experiencing the next couple of days.

I am now counting down the days until I go home. I miss my family so much and certainly miss all of the comforts and conveniences of modern life. I so desperately want to hold and hug my daughters. I long for them. This experience, although enlightening for sure, has been overwhelming. It's worse than I ever imagined it could be. All I can say is, "What next?"

What the Travel Brochure should have said:

Day 11: DZUGLA • 15,075 feet

From Dingboche the trail traverses through farmlands and meadows before continuing along the lateral moraine of the Khumbu Glacier. If you're lucky enough, you may be able to enjoy the views, since you had a day of rest to recover. You may still be dealing with dysentery, nausea, and more. And you certainly, by now, may be experiencing symptoms of altitude sickness. Make sure you drink plenty of fluids, since the altitude will cause severe headaches. And don't forget your Diamox. You must take it. If you don't, you risk having far more dangerous health problems. Your symptoms will worsen the higher you ascend. We will stop in Dzugla, a barren, beautiful wasteland. There's nothing here, but it works fine since going any higher today would be pushing it too far and might result in altitude sickness. At this point in the trek, you're beginning to seriously question why you came here. Don't think too much of it. Just grin and bear it, since you're getting much closer to the summit of Kala Patthar. You can't give up now.

9

MOUNTAIN SADNESS

*"Security is mostly a superstition. It does not exist in nature,
nor do the children of people as a whole experience it. . . .
Avoiding danger is no safer in the long run
than outright exposure. . . .
Life is either a daring adventure or nothing."*

-Helen Keller

11-18-04

TRAVEL BROCHURE DESCRIPTION:

Day 12: LOBUCHE • 16,175 feet

Today's trail continues along the lateral moraine of the Khumbu Glacier and passes by stone memorials for climbers who have perished on nearby summits. We follow the trail to Lobuche and camp just below the terminal moraine of a tributary glacier.

Trekking Company Menu:

Wakeup tea / Coffee / Hot Chocolates

B/F:
Porridge, Cram bled eggs, Pan Cake
Tea / Coffee / Chocolates

Lunch:
Juice, Brown Bread, Macaroni Salad, Tuna Fish, Cur kin Potato
Tea / Coffee / Chocolate

Refreshment
Tea / Coffee / Chocolates with Biscuits and snacks

Dinner:
Vegetable mushroom Pizza, Fruits Salad, Chicken Sausage Fry, Desert
Tea / Coffee/ Chocolates

5:45 P.M., town of Lobuche

I've been reading a book called *Mountains of the Mind: Adventures in Reaching the Summit*, by Robert McFarlane. My friends Karyn and Rich gave it to me as a gift prior to my departure. They thought it would be good idea to read it during the trek. I'm finding it fascinating – and helpful. There's a sentence that describes this trek in a nutshell: "These are matters of hard, steep, sharp rock and freezing snow, of extreme cold, of a vertigo so physical it can cramp your stomach and loosen your bowels, of hypertension, nausea, and frostbite, and of unspeakable beauty."

We woke up this morning in Dzugla with clouds smothering the tents. They were so dense we could reach out and touch them. I should have guessed even before I crawled out of my tent that it might be cloudy, based on the fact it was warmer than usual. It was a steamy hot twenty-four degrees Fahrenheit – unusually warm compared to what we have experienced on this journey in the early morning.

By 7:30 A.M., it started snowing and it continued for the next six hours, with a mix of wet snow and freezing rain during the entire hike up to Lobuche. Even though the temperature was warmer than usual, I was still feeling the chill in my newly scrawny body. I was lacking the solar energy I had relied on the other days to plow ahead and I was generally feeling pretty low. I continued to have a pounding headache the entire day. Except for a few brief moments, I've had it nonstop since I arrived in Namche Bazaar.

We hiked up another thousand feet today. The first seven hundred feet was unusually steep and tedious. It was disheartening and detrimental to my ability to stay optimistic. If I were hiking somewhere back in the U.S., I would view these difficult portions as a real challenge and get psyched to tackle them. I would put my head down and plow forward -- never once doubting my ability to succeed. Unfortunately, I am feeling defeated from being sick the past few days and operating at a profoundly reduced capacity.

Today was also the first day we were walking on snow – heavy, thick, wet snow. The trails each day up until now have simply been dirt, rocks, gravel, and embedded boulders. Adding wet snow to the mix made it exponentially more hazardous. Not only did the icy conditions and wet, slippery rocks make the trekking more dangerous, but the snow also masked the trail, making it immensely more difficult to assess what was underneath it. I therefore had to walk more slowly and carefully than ever before. I frequently hit the front of my boot on the hidden, entrenched stones, but quite luckily, with a hardened front toecap to prevent injury. Each time I hit my toe against a rock, a burst of electrical impulses and adrenaline rushed to my head, enabling me quickly to regain my balance and prevent me from falling.

I would get terribly discouraged if I looked ahead up the trail and saw a very steep portion coming up. I'd try to deal with it by minimizing the amount of times I snuck a peak, instead just looking at the snow and earth in front of my feet. There wasn't much else to see. I'd do this every fifteen minutes or so, and then look back in order to see how far I had progressed. Most of the time, I would shake my head in disgust, but I occasionally surprised myself by going much farther than I thought I had and I would experience a wonderful, yet brief sense of accomplishment.

As tough as this trek has been thus far, and as sick as I have been, I'm pleased I've made it to this point. No matter how difficult each day has been, I have continued to persevere. Even though I feel like garbage at the end of each day, I still have a great sense of accomplishment having gone the distance. And better yet, each day that passes is one day closer to the summit.

I know I've complained a great deal. And I know that based on all of my bitching the past few days, a person who didn't know any better would think I was climbing Mt. Everest, not Kala Patthar. If I were the only one feeling this way, I'd think for sure that something was seriously wrong with me. However, many others on this trek are feeling the exact same way I am. It's obvious that we're not hard core athletes or mountaineers – although Jack and Ian may be. We're just middle-aged, everyday guys and gals. We are probably more fit than most people in our respective age groups, but we are otherwise attempting something the difficulty of which we significantly underestimated. And compounding things, it's so much colder than it typically is at this time of year.

At the top of the first steep ridge we ascended there was a sobering sight, stone memorials honoring many of the climbers who have paid the ultimate price. There have been over two hundred deaths on and around Mt. Everest. Most of these individuals died attempting to summit her, above 8,000 meters, and many of them occurred after having reached the summit on their way back down. There were scores of tiny make-shift tombstones and a handful of much more elaborate ones. The most noticeable ones were for some of the more well known individuals who have died on the mountain. The largest by far was for Scott Fischer, the former owner of the Mountain Madness Trekking Company. He was one of a handful of climbers who perished in the great storm of 1996, profiled in Jon Krakauer's book *Into Thin Air*.

I read Krakauer's book a couple of times. The first time I read it was when it was first published in the late 90's. I considered it an amazing, yet incredibly sad story. The second time I read it, a few months prior to this trek, I tried to read it as more of an instruction manual. My goal was to try to glean any useful tips from it. Obviously, it wasn't overly effective for me from that perspective, since if I were smart enough, I would have backed out of the trip. There was certainly enough information to make it clear this was going to be an uncomfortable trip, but thanks to my poor decision-making skills, I am now living a nightmare. As much as Krakauer described so perfectly the awful conditions he experienced, his words, unfortunately, never hit home for me – especially since I was determined to come here.

Why couldn't I comprehend the gravity of the conditions here? I don't know. I'm not a doctor, a scientist, or a psychiatrist. I don't understand why so many people, present-company included, are incapable of reading the ample amount of information available regarding the poor conditions, disease, and dangers of high altitude trekking, and have it register in their brains. In my case was it willful blindness, since it was a life-long goal of mine not only to go on this trek, but also, possibly to climb Mt. Everest some day. It doesn't really matter. I'm here now and I need to make the best of it.

Stone Memorial for Scott Fischer, former owner of Mountain Madness, who died in the 1996 storm with many others.

Unless you have experienced this trek yourself, it's hard to imagine the true amount of discomfort involved. You never think it will be as bad or as dangerous or as unlucky for you, since most people falsely assume they'll be healthier, have better luck, or make wiser decisions than most others. And also, some people either have a general sense of invincibility, or, like me, are willfully ignorant. Unexpected things constantly happen in the mountains and oftentimes there isn't much you can do about it.

We continued on for a couple of miles, gaining a few hundred feet of altitude. With each step I took, it felt as if a vise was closing in against the sides of my head, slowly getting tighter and tighter. My week-long headache was growing worse from the cumulative effects of the altitude, the lack of water, the stress, the cold chill in my body, and particularly, from the tension in my neck and shoulders. This tension was created from my backpack, which was tugging at my shoulders, my neck, and my back all day long while trekking, and also from constantly staring at the ground. I hadn't thought about this prior to the trek, since I had never gone trekking for more than a few days in a row. However, I was quickly realizing that focusing on the ground for much of the day, for a full week, was surely exacerbating my symptoms.

It had been snowing nonstop from the point we arrived at the stone memorials all the way up to Lobuche. It was an absolutely dreadful-weather day. Thick, wet, heavy snowflakes were falling at a rapid clip. On top of everything else I was dealing with, the snow was like salt being poured on my wounds – those wounds being all of my maladies. We needed to be so careful trekking on the snowy terrain, keeping our eyes on the trail the entire time. We weren't missing any scenery, since it was impossible to see anything with the thick clouds surrounding us and the snow coming down.

I'm excited to say I am writing from a very small bedroom inside a tea lodge, where we are staying tonight. I feel protected from the elements in here. It's a wonderful, liberating feeling. The not-so-good news is there isn't any heat in the room, so it still feels like we are inside of a refrigerator. It is twenty-four degrees inside of my room. However, having the ability to stand up and stretch out is better than being in a small tent and having to maneuver like a contortionist.

I'm hoping it doesn't snow tomorrow, since it is supposed to be the toughest day of the trip, culminating with the summit of Kala Patthar. More important, if it's snowing, we won't have any view of Mt. Everest. That would be crushing, considering everything I've gone through on this trek.

We are at 16,000 feet now. Tomorrow we are going to climb more than 2,000 feet to the summit of Kala Patthar, known as the Black Rock (in Nepalese). I need to drink much more water tonight, and I need to eat as much as I possibly can at dinner in order to have the physical stamina needed to push my way to the summit tomorrow. Things are not looking good right now for a clear day, but I'm keeping my fingers crossed!

As I turned the page of the journal, I came across Reece's letter.

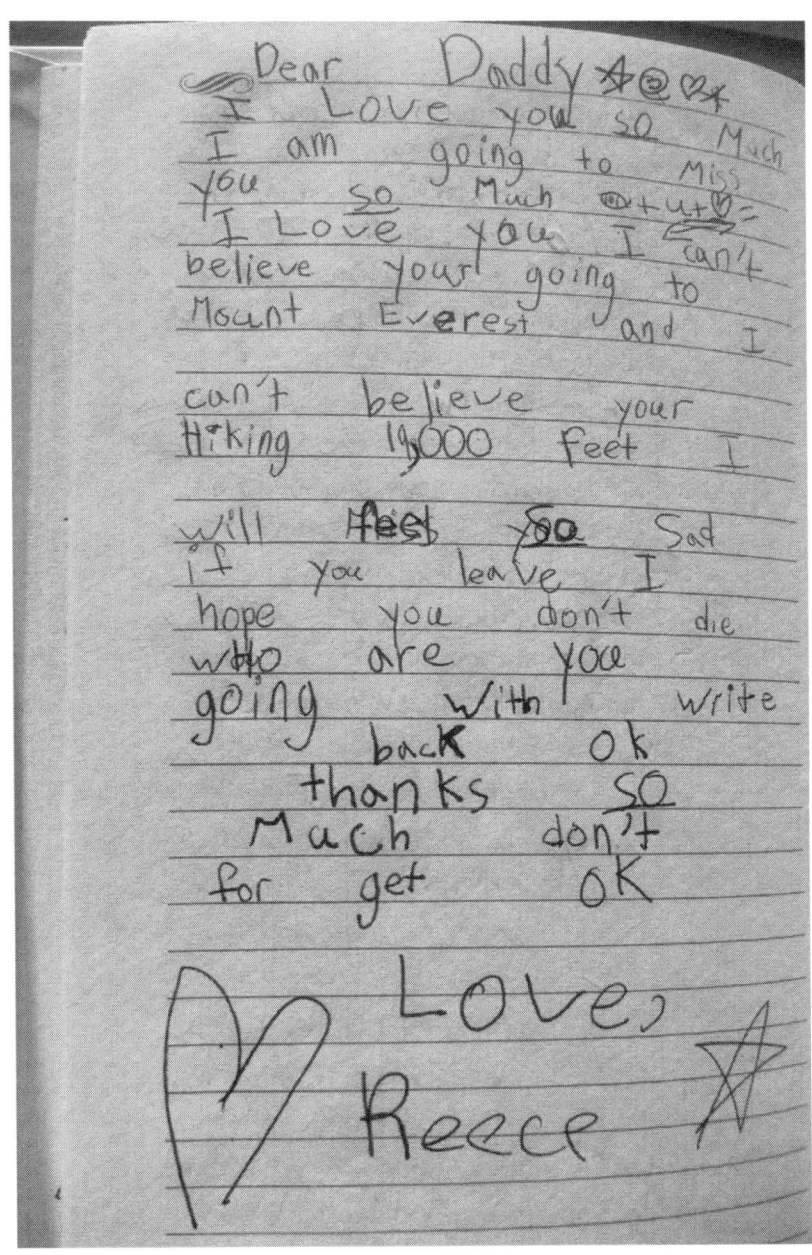

Dear Daddy ⭐@♥⭐
I Love you so Much
I am going to Miss
you so Much ♥+☺+♥=
I Love you I can't
believe your going to
Mount Everest and I

can't believe your
Hiking 19,000 feet I

will ~~feel~~ ~~so~~ Sad
if you leave I
hope you don't die
who are you
going with write
back ok
thanks so
Much don't
for get ok

Love,
Reece

I love you too Reece.

What the Travel Brochure should have said:

Day 12: LOBUCHE • 16,175 feet

Today's trail continues along the lateral moraine of the Khumbu Glacier and passes by stone memorials for climbers who have perished on nearby summits. Pay your respects. Many people have died attempting to summit Mt. Everest. You shouldn't worry, however, since most of these deaths have occurred above Base Camp. Regardless, you'll leave the memorials with plenty of thoughts to mull over while you are slowly working your way up to the summit. Be careful.

Town of Lobuche

10

ENDURANCE

"Never stop just because you feel defeated. The journey to the other side is attainable only after great suffering."

-Santosh Kalwar

11-19-04

TRAVEL BROCHURE DESCRIPTION:

Day 13: GORAK SHEP • 17,000 feet

After an early morning start, we ascend Kala Patthar (18,450 feet) and enjoy famous views of the Himalayas, without having to climb Everest. That evening we camp beneath Kala Patthar at Gorak Shep.

Trekking Company Menu:

Wakeup tea / Coffee / Hot Chocolates

B/F:
Corn-flakes, Potato Omlet, Hot Cake
Tea / Coffee / Chocolates

Lunch:
Juice, Chapati, Salad, Beans, Cheese, Sardine Fish
Tea / Coffee / Chocolates

Refreshment
Tea / Coffee / Chocolates with Biscuits and snacks

Dinner:
Rubi Olin, Tomato Sausage, French Fri, Boil Vegetables, Fruits
Tea / Coffee / Chocolates

5:50 P.M., town of Gorak Shep

We were scheduled to awaken at 4:45 AM this morning if the forecast called for it to be sunny, in order to start the trek early. We then would head toward Gorak Shep, our last acclimatization stop and the original Everest Base Camp location many years ago, at 17,000 feet, where we'd be camping for two nights. Gorak Shep translates as "dead ravens" in Nepalese, since there is no vegetation at all. Once in Gorak Shep, we would then drop off some of the extra gear from our backpacks that we wouldn't need for the climb to the top of Kala Patthar. We would then immediately head toward the summit. If by some likely chance it happened to be cloudy at 4:45 A.M., or if it was snowing, then we were going to start the hike later in the day and possibly summit the next day.

By 5:00 A.M., nobody had knocked on my door, even though I was wide awake from nervous anticipation. I assumed the weather wasn't cooperating. I waited impatiently, staring at my watch every few minutes. Finally, at 6:30 A.M., the porters knocked on my door and asked me to be ready a half hour later for breakfast.

It wasn't until after breakfast, however, that we were informed the sun was finally breaking through the clouds and it was a "go." Even though we were starting out a couple of hours later than planned, we were going to attempt to go for the summit. If the weather turned for the worse, we could always stop at Gorak Shep today and attempt the summit tomorrow.

As usual, it took us close to an hour to get our gear ready after breakfast. We knew what we had to do, but we were all dragging like snails. Although we were well aware today was the big day, there was zero enthusiasm amongst anyone in the group. There wasn't a single person who was acting as the cheerleader. It all seemed a bit anticlimactic, after everything we had been through. We were cold, hungry, tired, and sick – a pathetic-looking bunch of trekkers, nothing like the group of eager-beavers ready to conquer the Himalayas just nine days earlier. It was if we had already lost the war.

We were trying to get some kind of weather and temperature forecast, in order to figure out the necessary gear we should be carrying. This was crucially important, especially at this altitude, and it wasn't easy to get it right. Even if I know it's going to be cold, I won't bring along many layers with me in my backpack, since I also know I'll be working hard physically and working up a sweat, which has been the case every single day except for the "rest" days. I always carry a windproof and waterproof North Face shell, since it is lightweight and does a great job of protecting me from the elements. It has been a staple for me the entire trek. Other than the shell however, everything else I carry in my pack is determined by the forecast each morning, along with the distance we'll be trekking and the altitude we'll be climbing each day.

All along, I've been dependent on the guides getting the forecast correct. If they predict moderate weather and then the weather turns out to be much colder than expected, I'll pay a hefty price. However, if it ends up being warmer than forecasted, I'll end up carrying needless extra pounds on my back. Every extra pound at this altitude, on top of my poor physical health, feels like I'm lugging an additional cinderblock.

Lorraine informed us it was supposed to clear up completely within the hour and be sunny all day, with the temperature in the high 20's. It sounded like we were going to get lucky. We packed up our gear and all met in the tea lodge dining area, where the smoke from the yak dung was filling the room.

We left Lobuche at 8:30 A.M. and hiked mostly as a team, except for the "fast guys," through some of the most amazing terrain covered in the smoothest blanket of white snow I've ever seen. It was evident the vast area we hiked through in the morning had received a fresh coating of snow last night. Even though I was exhausted, I did my best to enjoy the glorious views.

I spent the first hour or so talking with George. It was the first real honest-to-goodness conversation I had had with anyone on this entire trek. We discussed our respective kids, their ages, their likes and dislikes, and more. His kids are a few years younger than mine. If you had listened to the conversation, you could have told we were proud dads. I asked him about his wife and her comfort level with him going on this trek. He said she had no issues with him taking this trip, as well as others. He has already climbed Mt. Kilimanjaro. I was glad to hear it, since I have thought about climbing it in the future. I grilled him on all sorts of questions related to that climb and he answered them all, making it clear that it was an easier trek than this one, since it is much shorter in distance and time, even though it is approximately a thousand feet higher in altitude. Kilimanjaro also lacks the peaks and valleys of the Himalayas, which was music to my ears.

I could see a few other trekking groups on the trail, way out in the distance. It was the first time since being here that we were in such a massive, wide open valley, probably two miles long, alongside the glacier. From my vantage point, it appeared as if those trekkers far off in the distance were going to arrive at the end of the horizon and then just drop off the mountain. Since I've trekked frequently, I expected that once I arrived at that point there would be plenty more hiking still to come. And I was right. The trail just kept going…and going.

Besides the people on the trail, all I saw were snow-covered peaks and monolithic, jagged mountains and boulders for miles. The sky was a luminous blue, unlike any I had ever seen before. I couldn't have wished for a nicer day and a more pristine landscape. The views along the entire trail were exquisite, except for the sight of the muddy path created by the hordes of trekkers. It was fortunate for us that we had gotten off to a late start. Others who had ascended before us had cleared some of the snow from the trail, making it easier for us to see what we were walking on.

We ascended one thousand feet in about three hours, walking a few miles and continuously witnessing miraculous views, which became more magical with each and every step. We passed a large bird perched on a boulder, with a heavy gray and white coat of feathers, a pure white underbelly and a pointy, clawed orange beak, which a porter said was a snow goose, although it didn't look anything like a snow goose. It was a magnificent creature, with the snow-white landscape behind it, just sitting still within a few feet of us, taking in the rays, enjoying the day and possibly waiting for some scraps of food.

As taxing as the trek was on my body and as difficult as it was on my lungs, it was still manageable because I did my best to not think about it. I would gaze at the pure beauty all around me and be distracted from the discomfort. After the first hour or two of trekking, everyone was silent – except for their heavy panting – because of the lack of oxygen…and presumably their awe.

I could feel and hear my heart beating rapidly inside of me. Strangely, it added to the intense beauty. The views, along with my heavy beating heart, left me under a spell, as if I was on a powerful, psychedelic drug. Maybe it was something like a "runner's high," which I had so often heard about but never actually experienced while running. Maybe I was experiencing a "trekkers high." I was so engrossed with every peak I passed and hill I climbed that I was able to block out any of my discomforts. I was completely fixated on the ethereal beauty all around me.

I don't consider myself a spiritual person, but I do firmly believe that some people are capable of reaching a higher level of enlightenment, whether by means of meditation or some other mechanism. I thought that, just maybe, I had experienced this feeling today.

My mind continued to wander all morning. I felt small, hiking in all of this vast beauty, like a speck of matter. The valley was so enormous, and yet it was just one of thousands in the Himalayas. It was humbling knowing these mountains have existed for millions of years and that they'll continue to be here for millions more after I'm long gone. I was wondering if there would be other trekkers walking the same paths a million years from now, and if so, would they be humans or some other creatures – having evolved over time naturally or because of an unnatural event, such as a nuclear war, which I regrettably believe may occur at some point in the not-too-distant future.

I realized I had been given a gift, something to cherish for the rest of my life. I was appreciating how truly precious life is and I was thinking more and more about how I needed to refocus my priorities back home. Have I been a good enough father to my girls? Was I around for them often enough? Had I worked too hard for too many years, for the sake of a paycheck? Was it all worth it? These thoughts flooded my brain during much of the morning. Since I still had a crippling headache, and I had accordingly been popping large quantities of aspirin, I intermittently wondered if the aspirin was causing me to feel so enlightened. It wasn't like me to be so self-reflective, but I enjoyed the process and I think it was good for me.

After the brutal hike, we finally reached Gorak Shep around noon. Although I was utterly fatigued, I was ecstatic I had made it without any major calamities. Yet I knew the truly demanding part of the day was yet to come.

Hiking from Lobuche to Gorak Shep at approximately 16,500 feet.

I had been sweating all morning from the strenuous effort, and now my body was getting cold as we stood around for a few minutes. Although the sun continued to shine with a great intensity, it was bitterly cold and windy at this altitude – much more adverse conditions than I had ever experienced. But I had never been at 17,000 feet above sea level before, and I had no idea what the conditions would be like, nor did I know how the altitude would affect me. This was unexplored territory for me.

I needed to keep moving or I was going to freeze. Lorraine also didn't want to wait too long to head up to the summit, since the mid-afternoon weather is terribly unpredictable. We eliminated all things from our backpacks that were deemed unnecessary, in order to lighten our load. After taking just ten minutes to catch our breath, we headed toward the summit of Kala Patthar.

Kala Patthar is nothing but a huge brown dirt hill. It increases steeply approximately 1,200 feet in altitude from Gorak Shep. There is no snow on it at all, although I'm not sure why, since there is snow almost everywhere else I looked. It's not an aesthetically appealing mountain. The lower half of the mountain is mostly loose dirt and scree, which creates an awful, lung-clogging cloud of dust as it is trampled upon. The top half of the mountain is covered in big stones and ever larger boulders, the closer you ascend toward the summit.

Most of the team had separated within minutes of starting out. We became more spread apart as time passed, based on our respective physical capabilities. The "fast guys" had departed for the summit long ago. Luckily, it didn't matter that we had separated, since there was only one, plainly visible trail, for most of the way – straight up to the top.

Unlike the climb this morning from Lobuche to Gorak Shep, which was difficult enough, the climb to the summit of Kala Patthar was hellishly demanding given the steep pitch of the mountain. This, combined with my poor health, the intense sun, my pounding head, the difficulty breathing at such a high altitude, and the lack of sleep and carbohydrates the past few days, created a powerful and dangerous set of conditions that overwhelmed me.

Every breath I took was a challenge -- a desperate gasp for air. I felt as if someone had stuffed a sock in my mouth and plugged up my nose. My asthma surely increased the difficulty. Every inch forward was a struggle. The higher I ascended, the slower I moved. I took one step every few seconds. I was more light-headed than I had ever been before, and the farther I climbed, the worse it became.

I was attempting to remember the symptoms Lorraine had described regarding HAPE and HACE. We had gained significant altitude pretty quickly over the past two days. Lacking the Diamox, which I had stopped taking because of my constant need to urinate while I was briefly on it, I was beginning to experience real signs of altitude sickness. I wasn't able to think clearly enough to know whether these were just random concerns or whether there was a real danger to what I was experiencing. I felt as if I was "lost in space."

Despite my lightheadedness, I just kept slogging forward. I was making my way toward the summit with a glacially slow crawl. I had come way too far not to get this done. I kept telling myself that I had to finish. I was so close. I couldn't give up now!

The sun was dangerously powerful, intensifying my already unbearable headache. It felt like there was a giant magnifying glass directly above me, with the sun's rays focused on my head, burning a hole in my brain. My face felt like it was under a broiler. My insides were overheated from the herculean effort I was exerting on each step. Although I was at a very high altitude in below freezing temperatures, it felt like I was in Death Valley in one hundred and twenty degree temperature. My body was using every ounce of energy from every carb I had ingested on the trek, and then some. It was working in overdrive, in order to turn anything it could find inside of me into energy, so I could continue on.

As I came closer and closer to the summit, the wind was blowing ever more fiercely. I kept moving, ignoring the strong gusts that constantly threatened to knock me down. Huge boulders, embedded almost everywhere near the summit, were appearing with greater and greater frequency as I ascended. I had to do a significant amount of scrambling, utilizing my hands as much as my feet, to continue higher.

I was probably thirty yards from the summit when I suddenly became profoundly lightheaded. At that very moment, as I was standing upright and balanced on a large rock, I started to sway backwards. I should have had enough sense to know I was about to fall and to do something about it. There should have been a warning over the loudspeaker in my head saying "DANGER, DAVID SCHACHNE, DANGER." However, the speaker system had short-circuited. The sun had fried the electrical panel in my brain, causing it overheat and lose the ability to communicate with my body. I had been overcome by heat and exhaustion, and I wasn't processing any vital information.

I was continuing to topple backward. Although it seemed to me it was happening in slow motion, it wasn't. For one millisecond, I thought I was imagining I was falling because of my dizziness, but I wasn't. It was real, it was happening, and I was in trouble. I had spent the past nine days working harder physically than ever before, and experiencing more anguish and despair than I ever had and hopefully ever will. Yet, after all of it, there was at this moment a very strong possibility I was about to get seriously hurt.

Miraculously, an angel appeared out of nowhere. It was an angel in the form of a Sherpa. I felt him support me from behind and push me back into an upright position. I have no idea if he had been trailing me the whole time or if he had suddenly noticed I wasn't doing well and decided to "watch my back." Regardless, it was perfect timing. I have no idea if I would have taken a bad fall if he hadn't been there to catch me, but it seems all too likely.

I stood there for a second, trying to come to grips with what had just occurred – as much as I possibly could at the time since I was still, to some degree, in la-la land. The altitude was affecting my ability to think clearly. I took a few deep breaths, regained my composure, chugged some water, and then climbed the last few yards, step by step and boulder by boulder, to the crowded summit.

Although I was, of course, glad to have reached the summit, and although I certainly felt a huge relief, the true joy of it hadn't hit me just yet. My body and brain were still going through too much, both physically and emotionally, to fully appreciate what I had accomplished. I took a minute to stand there and breathe, as best as I could, with the harsh winds still blowing hard.

After a few more moments, my brain started functioning again. I had come back to my senses. And my brain couldn't believe what my eyes were seeing. A sudden chill ran down my spine the likes of which I had never experienced before, and it had nothing to do with the frigid weather.

I had seen the Himalayas in pictures many times, but nothing could compare to being there. It was so vivid, so three dimensional, so fantastic. Some of the tallest mountains in the world lay before my eyes, including Everest, Pomuri, Nuptse, Lhotse, and many others, stretched out into the heavens. The sky was a dazzling, deep-ocean blue. The bleached-white clouds in the background looked like perfectly shaped cotton balls. How could something so absolutely spectacular be so real?

This is why I came here. There has never been anything more visually beautiful to me than a majestic mountain range. And there has never been a mountain I longed to see in person more than Everest. I could not believe I was standing there, feeling as if I could reach out and touch her. It was hard to believe Mt. Everest was still 11,000 feet higher than where I was standing at that moment, and that it would require another three to four weeks of acclimatization in order to attempt to summit it.

Few people on the planet will ever have the opportunity to experience what I did today. Even fewer will witness it as I did on such a perfectly beautiful day. I had pushed myself as much as I possibly could to get this far, risking my safety and my health, and I was rewarded in the end for my efforts. For me, it was a feat of epic of proportion. I will forever hold this memory of being there in my heart.

It was cold at the summit, yet it wasn't because of the temperature. It was probably a moderate twenty-five degrees or so, maybe even warmer. Rather, the cold chill was cutting into my bones because all of my layers were soaking wet – as if I had fallen into a swimming pool – from the sweaty ascent. The wind was blowing violently, causing a deadly wind-chill effect, piercing my skin and biting into my bones. There were prayer flags at the top of the summit, making thunderously loud noises as they fluttered and flailed in the powerful winds. I could barely stand up straight as the intense winds threatened to pry me off the mountaintop. I was doing my best to fight it – using whatever leverage I could with the minimal strength I had left in my leg muscles. I slowly and cautiously moved around, taking in the phenomenal views.

I crept over to the backside of the mountain to see the view on the opposite side of the summit from the one we had climbed. It was an entirely different scene from what I had just experienced. Instead of a few of the tallest mountains in the world sitting right in front of me, the backside of Kala Patthar exposed a panorama of mountains for countless miles – a truly mesmerizing scene. There was a massive expanse, basically an ocean of hills, valleys, mountains, and tall peaks for as far as the eye could see. It went against all logic that anything like it, so amazingly awesome, could exist.

No matter how ill I felt, I wasn't going to let that get in the way of relishing this brief moment. Still, in the back of my mind, I knew I needed to get down the mountain and back to the campsite – and it wasn't going to be easy.

Plenty of climbing accidents happen not prior to, but after reaching the summit. Climbers become overtired, having exhausted all their energy to get to the summit. And others simply get careless. Regardless, I knew I had a long trip back down and I was well aware of just how bad of a condition I was in. So, after taking nine full days to reach the summit, I stayed there for a total of five minutes before heading back down. Besides, if I hadn't made a conscious decision to leave, the wind would have decided for me anyway.

It was a treacherous hike back to the campsite, and a monumental challenge to keep from slipping on the loose scree. Combined with the steep pitch of the mountain, the scree created an ice-like surface. I was trying my hardest to prevent gravity from forcing me down the mountain too quickly, and possibly causing me to slip and fall. The sun was brighter than ever, reflecting off the snow-covered peaks surrounding me. It was baking my face, even with my high altitude SPF 50 sun block covering the exposed skin, and worsening my agonizing migraine. I couldn't take my eyes off the trail for a split second, because I would have ended up tripping and rolling down the mountainside. The required concentration of focusing on the ground, with my already tense neck sharply bent downward, and the sun broiling my face, resulted in my brain feeling like a spike was being driven through it.

Despite it all, I finally made it back to Gorak Shep, and quietly thanked God.

Today was physically the hardest day of my life, a true test of my ability to endure. It was a towering accomplishment for me to reach the summit of Kala Patthar. Never in my life have I pushed myself as much as I did today. Never in my life would I ever have anticipated how physically demanding this day was going to be and the hardship I would have to bear. Yet for all of the pain and absolute misery I have experienced, it has all finally paid off. I was triumphant.

I am elated right now…on top of the world. Well, not quite, but close enough. It is the first time on this entire trek that I feel true joy and happiness. My body has been put through the grinder on this trek, by nature, by my inadequacies, illness, filth, and more. Yet through it all, and as much as I was close to giving up, I made it. I feel great knowing I accomplished my goal.

Everyone was successful today except for Fernando. He wasn't feeling well at all and didn't want to risk his health any further. I felt bad for him, but he seemed fine with his decision. At least he told us so. The rest of us all reached the summit at different times throughout the day. We didn't congregate as a team until late this afternoon when every one of us had finally arrived back at the mess tent at Gorak Shep. As thrilled as I was to have conquered the mountain, you wouldn't have ever known it by looking at me, or anyone else on the team for that matter. Instead of jumps for joy, high-fives, and loud cheers, we congratulated each other by simply shaking hands and exchanging soft whispers of congratulations. We were all too ill and tired to do anything else. It was a telling scene.

As I sit here now, it feels so good, yet I still hurt so much. My body is absolutely wasted, unquestionably void of any shred of strength. The colossal headache I have had all afternoon is still with me and is still so terribly painful.

For those individuals who are physically, mentally, and emotionally capable of summiting Mt. Everest, it has to be one of the greatest joys of their lives. I wish I had the DNA required to go for it one day. However, after experiencing this living nightmare, I am reasonably confident I will never make it to the top of Everest. It bothers me to say this, since I've always believed anything is possible through hard work, dedication, and perseverance. However, there are just too many physical limitations preventing me from reaching the summit of the highest point on earth. Even if I improved my physical condition to the point where I was in the best physical shape of my life, it would make no difference. Without the ability to believe I can actually make it, it wouldn't matter if my body could handle the physical effort. I would need both to prevail. Climbing Everest had at one point been a goal of mine, but I'm crossing it off the bucket list.

As much as reaching the summit of Everest would be an accomplishment of a lifetime, I no longer have any desire to do it. I'd be risking way too much. My life and my family are so much more important to me than one mountain. Making it as far as I did today will have to be good enough. It is good enough. I am euphoric...and I am done.

There's another quote from *Mountains of the Mind* that accurately describes my attitude. It's from Edward Whymper, a climber who in 1865 was the sole survivor of a hiking accident in which four of his companions died after summiting the Matterhorn. He provided an epitaph for his friends, one appropriate for this trip, and for high altitude trekking in general: "Climb if you will, but remember that courage and strength are naught without prudence, and a momentary negligence may destroy the happiness of a lifetime. Do nothing in haste, look well to each step, and from the beginning think what may be the end." This quote is on a plaque at the top of Mt. Washington in New Hampshire, which I've climbed a few times and where over 100 people have died from falls, hypothermia, and other causes. The plaque has been there for many years, but I first noticed it only after going on this trek and reading my book.

I sit here now, feeling sick to my stomach, lightheaded, and nursing the worst migraine of my life. I have expended every ounce of energy I had. I have no more to give. I can't wait to hold Faith and the girls in my arms. I yearn to be warm and comfortable and out of harm's way in my own home. I can't wait to get the fuck out of here.

What the Travel Brochure should have said:

Day 13: GORAK SHEP • 17,000 feet

If all goes according to plan, we ascend Kala Patthar. It will be the most challenging, grueling day of your life. The altitude will cause such an incapacitating headache you will think somebody hit you on the head with a sledge hammer – repeatedly. Today will also be the most dangerous day, since you will be most vulnerable to injury. We don't mean to scare you, but we need to be honest. So be careful. That said, if you make it to the top, you will have accomplished the feat of your lifetime and will experience views of the Himalayas that will leave you in awe.

View of Mount Everest, upper left. Picture taken from the summit of Kala Patthar. Mt. Nuptse (right) appears taller due to it being closer to Kala Patthar

The Western view from the summit of Kala Patthar, facing the opposite direction from Mt. Everest.

A view of the summit of Kala Patthar (center) with prayer flags blowing in the wind, with Mt. Pumori in the background.

CHAPTER TEN: ENDURANCE

11

SPENT

"Of all the paths a man could strike into, there is, at any given moment, a best path... A thing which, here and now, it were of all things wisest for him to do... To find this path, and walk in it, is the one thing needful for him."

-Thomas Carlyle

11-20-04

TRAVEL BROCHURE DESCRIPTION:

Day 14: EVEREST BASE CAMP • 17,575 feet

Today we will continue our trek to Everest Base Camp, located at the foot of the Khumbu Icefall. We'll spend the day at Everest/Lhotse Base Camp, giving you a chance to thoroughly explore this historic area.

Trekking Company Menu:

Wakeup tea / Coffee / Hot Chocolates

B/F:
Muslee, Tomato Omlet, Donut
Tea / Coffee / Chocolates

Lunch:
Juice, Khopse (*not sure what this is, but Khopse was the name of one of the Porters. I hope they didn't eat him for lunch! At least I know I didn't since I didn't have any meat*),
Potato Salad, Read Beans, Cane Meat,
Tea / Coffee / Chocolates

Refreshment
Tea / Coffee / Chocolates **with Biscuits and snacks**

Dinner:
Vegetable Mushroom Chopsey (*translation: Chop Suey*), Spring roll, Sweet & Sour Chicken
Desert Tea / Coffee / Chocolates

6:00 A.M., Gorak Shep

I 'm hoping my fingers don't get frostbitten while I write in my journal this morning. I'm sitting in my tent with most of my body inside of my sleeping bag after being awake all night. It was an unusually awful night. I know it's hard to believe I can say this after all I've been through thus far. If you asked me yesterday if things could have been any worse, I would have surely told you "no." But it was worse, a different kind of worse from what I've experienced until now.

As we were eating dinner last night, which for me meant soup and French fries, and recovering from the summit climb, the temperature was dropping minute by minute. It was already in the single digits.

I had put on my expedition down parka for the very first time. I had brought it with me even though I didn't think I would actually be using it on the trip. It wasn't supposed to be so brutally cold this time of the year. The jacket is very bulky, probably weighing close to four pounds. It is nothing like the latest lightweight gear now utilized for climbing in the Himalayas. It is a jacket I had received from a business customer when I worked in the feather and down business with my father twenty years ago. I think I have worn it once or twice since I've owned it. It was meant to be worn going up to Mt. Everest at 29,035 feet, not at 17,000 feet at Gorak Shep. I brought it with me strictly for an "emergency" situation. And that's what it was last night. Oddly, it hadn't dawned on me to wear the parka earlier during the trek, particularly during the cold evenings. I'm not sure why, except that I had mentally noted before I left that it was to only be used during emergencies. Clearly, my brain has not been functioning optimally at these high altitudes.

The winds picked up significantly as the evening progressed last night. It was the first time since the trek began that there were wildly strong gusts blowing throughout the entire evening. Of course, it has been consistently cold each and every evening, but prior to last night, there were never high winds, creating an even more brutal environment.

My fingers became numb as I attempted to spoon the hot broth into my mouth at dinner. The winds were making eerie, whistling sounds that echoed through the high valley. Nobody was speaking. I was shivering like a human vibrator, my teeth chattering non-stop. My head still felt like someone had swung a baseball bat at it. I was at a new all-time low. It wasn't even 7:00 PM, but I decided I needed to get out of the mess tent and into my sleeping bag as fast as possible. Although I had conquered Kala Patthar, she had gotten her retribution on me by beating my body, and particularly my head, to a pulp.

Until last night, I've been sleeping in multiple layers inside of my sleeping bag and liner, but without my heavy parka. This had been sufficient in keeping me reasonably warm while sleeping (or attempting to sleep.) But last night, I was still freezing cold inside of the sleeping bag and thus had to wear my expedition parka as well.

The pounding headache I had had all day yesterday during my summit climb got progressively worse throughout the evening. The extra-strength aspirin I basically overdosed on by taking it every few hours, to no avail, contained caffeine. Since I never have caffeine, anything caffeinated has an immediate and long lasting effect on me. As a result of this, as well as the altitude, I couldn't fall sleep. It was torture.

I tossed and turned continuously, for hours, which wasn't easy with all of the layers I was wearing. At around midnight, my bladder felt like it was going to burst. I had had to urinate for a few hours, but I held it in since I didn't want to get out of my cocoon. I finally managed to force myself out of the sleeping bag and took a leak in my pee bottle. I foolishly tried to convince myself that if I urinated, I'd be able to get some sleep. Unfortunately, I did not.

A few minutes after I returned to my sleeping bag, the wind gusts began picking up significantly and were blowing against the tent and the tarp violently. The ferocious winds were howling like a pack of wolves. Within minutes, the force of the strong gusts caused one or more of the spikes holding down the tarp to come loose. One side of the tarp was flopping up and down, repeatedly crashing into the tent and causing huge earsplitting thuds. My headache became excruciating.

It fortunately wasn't very long before the porters had heard the constant pounding of my tarp. They weren't willing to leave it in an unstable condition. I'm not sure if it was bothering them enough to do something about it or if they wanted to make sure I was safe. I would assume the latter, based on everything I've experienced to date. The fact that the porters were watching out for us in these blizzard-like conditions clearly demonstrates how much they had our safety in mind at all times.

They had always done a solid job of securing the tent in the ground at each site where we camped, but some spots were more stubborn than others. And they surely didn't anticipate these high winds. So, at some point around 1:00 A.M., they had to fix my tent and re-pound the spikes into the ground. I can't even imagine how difficult it must have been for them doing this in the middle of the night, with gale force winds and with below-zero degree wind-chill temperatures. I could hear them screaming to each other, communicating over the wailing of the winds, while banging away at the spikes. They were out there for about ten minutes. I felt helpless as they did their job, but happy for them when it was finally done, knowing they were safely back in their tents.

I lay awake all night long, counting down the hours until dawn, and hoping I would fall asleep in the process. No such luck. After realizing it was a futile effort, I eventually started praying that the time would fly by and then the sun would quickly rise, and the harsh weather would subside. I was wishing for another beautiful, sunny, calm day as it had been yesterday.

I was terrified of the thought of possibly having to take a crap. I couldn't even begin to fathom how awful it would have been if I had to leave my tent in the middle of the night in the unrelenting weather. My extremities would have certainly become frostbitten. I think I may have willed myself into not having to go. Frankly, I'm not even sure if the outhouse would have been standing there even if I did have to go, since the porters had set up a small makeshift one earlier that afternoon. It was basically a 3 foot x 3 foot x 6 foot tent with a giant hole in the floor, dug by the porters, to capture our waste.

At around 3:00 AM, I looked at the temperature gauge on my watch and it read ten degrees inside my tent. I got out of my sleeping bag again to pee in my pee bottle, and discovered my pee had frozen solid from three hours earlier. For the very first time on the trek, I didn't have to worry about my pee bottle accidentally spilling on my gear when I opened it.

Late afternoon

At 7:00 A.M. this morning, the cooking staff came by my tent to make sure I was awake.

Duh! The winds were still wild, blowing the staff around like leaves in a November nor'easter.

Inside my now secure tarp, the staff placed the usual hot water bowl for me to brush my teeth along with the mug of hot water to drink. It was nerve-racking going about my morning rituals with the temperature so low. I hesitated opening my tent flap to reach for the hot water, since I didn't want to let any cold air into my tent. However, I knew it would be worth it once I could get a grip on the boiling water and gulp it down. When I finally did, it felt extraordinary. It was a truly stupendous feeling. I never thought I could get high on hot water, but I did. I felt it make contact with every internal organ it touched as it travelled down my digestive tract.

We were scheduled to hike to Everest Base Camp today, seven hours round-trip from Gorak Shep. We all went to breakfast around 8:00 AM. It was five degrees when I stepped out of my tent. The temperature alone would have been more than enough to make me uncomfortable, but the worst part was the fierce winds, which had not subsided at all. The powerful winds effectively made the temperature feel like it was minus ten to twenty degrees. It felt like thousands of razor blades cutting into my face. It wasn't easy getting to the mess tent with the wind blowing so forcefully. I fought hard, angling my body forward and utilizing every muscle in my skinny legs. It looked as if I was at a football training camp pushing an invisible sled of tackling dummies.

At breakfast, there was dead silence. Nobody uttered a word. Everyone was simply too frozen, their minds numb and their bodies spent. We were beaten, battered, and wasted from the living nightmare that this trip has been to us. We all sat there attempting to put some food in our mouths, as if we were helpless geriatric patients. We slowly, achingly reached for anything hot – oatmeal, hot water, coffee, or tea. Nobody was looking forward to starting the day. It was hard to believe we actually paid to live through this torment. We are truly idiots!

For anyone attempting to head to Base Camp this morning, the reward would be a view of the Khumbu Icefall. The penalty, however, would be putting oneself through living hell for another twenty-four hours. Not only would we be spending seven hours going to Base Camp and back, in this god-awful weather, but we would also have to spend another night eating and sleeping at Gorak Shep in these frigid conditions. And I'd have to go through another evening of sub-zero temperatures, intense winds, and incapacitating headaches. This was an agonizing thought, and difficult to accept after all I had been through. I didn't think I could take any more of this.

All of a sudden, as if someone was hearing my prayers, three of the guys in our group, Teddy, Mitch, and Fernando, approached Lorraine. Looking like wounded dogs, they asked her if they could head down to Pheriche, instead of going to Everest Base Camp today. Teddy whispered three of the truest words ever spoken with as much energy as he could muster, "This isn't fun."

Lorraine was the sole person responsible for our safety. If some of the trekkers didn't want to go any farther, she certainly wasn't going to force them. She acknowledged the weather was

177

unusually cold for this time of year and said she understood how they felt. She told them it was their decision. I was wondering if she actually would have preferred not to go as well, but she didn't have a choice, since she was guiding the group. As long as there were some people who wanted to go Base Camp, and she felt it was safe to do so, she was required to lead them there.

She asked the rest of our group if anyone else was interested in joining the three guys heading down to Pheriche. Her words were music to my ears. Before she could even finish asking, I raised my hand without saying a word. I looked around and was amazed that none of the other eight team members had raised their hands. I was shocked. More power to them, I thought, but at least my prayers had been answered.

I asked Lorraine what we'd be missing by not going. I was hoping her answer would be what I wanted to hear. It was good enough. "Not much – just a crashed helicopter, old tents, lots of trash, and of course, a view of the Khumbu Icefall."

The chance to see the Khumbu Icefall was one of the reasons I had signed up for the trek. At approximately 18,000 feet, and slightly beyond Everest Base Camp on the way up South Col route toward the summit of Mt. Everest, the icefall is both beautiful and deadly. A large number of fatalities on Everest have occurred there, more than any other part of the route, if I'm not mistaken.

The icefall is part of the Khumbu Glacier, which has been known to move down the mountain at a very fast rate relative to most other glaciers. This movement creates hazardous conditions, including dangerously deep and wide crevasses, as well as the tumbling of gigantic blocks of ice, known as seracs, down the mountainside. Many climbers have been killed by these seracs breaking apart and falling on them.

I've known about the icefall for many years and had a strong desire to see it based on how wondrously beautiful, yet dangerous, it is. Just the same, it didn't take me long to decide to head down and take a pass on this once-in-a-lifetime opportunity. I might have given it more thought had I felt even slightly healthier, but my condition had continued to deteriorate. Reaching the summit of Kala Patthar, above Base Camp, is a huge enough accomplishment for me, and will have to suffice.

All that said, I felt l I was missing out on something. It was a lousy feeling. Later in the day, after having plenty of time to think about my decision, I tried to figure out why it was bothering me so much. I came to the conclusion it was my pride. For most of my life, I have accomplished whatever I set out to do. This was the first time I could recall that I had wanted to do something so badly and didn't. I felt as if I had failed. I had wanted to see Base Camp and the Khumbu Icefall for so long. It was a feeling of defeat for me to not be able to go this one last distance, after having travelled thousands of miles and having put myself through all of this suffering.

But as "Dirty Harry" Callahan used to say, "A man's got to know his limitations." I had finally acknowledged mine. And the more I thought about, the more I realized that while seeing Base Camp was most certainly a strong desire of mine, in the true scheme of things, it really wasn't that important.

My body has physically been through hell the past nine days. I am in bad shape. I have had enough. If I thought there was even a slight possibility I might still want to climb Mt. Everest at some future date, then maybe, just maybe, I would have considered pushing myself beyond my limit today. But I realized yesterday, with certainty, that I will never pursue that insane dream.

Eight trekkers and the two guides, Lorraine and Dakotah, left for Base Camp this morning, heading off into ferocious winds, with some Sherpas of course. Teddy, Mitch, Fernando and I, headed down towards Pheriche, into similarly vicious winds, but at least we were descending.

Just twenty-four hours earlier, we came up the mountain into Gorak Shep in beautiful, sunny, mild conditions. Today's treacherous weather was the complete opposite. As I've known for years, this is what the weather conditions are like with high altitude climbing, and it's why so many people perish in the mountains. Nature is unpredictable and far more powerful than any man or woman – regardless of how driven the person may be. There's no contest, no matter how many movies we watch to convince ourselves otherwise.

Even so, I can understand how climbers may make poor decisions on Everest. First, you can't think clearly at all. I witnessed this at altitudes that pale in comparison. Second, it's a sense of pride, especially if climbing Mt. Everest has been a lifelong goal. People let their guards down when egos get in the way. And last, if you spend a full six weeks working your way toward the summit of Everest, which is what most people generally need to do, fighting all sorts of personal battles along the way, and then you're within shouting distance of the summit, it would be incredibly difficult to stop and turn around.

Whether by pure chance or fate, if I hadn't read the book *Mountains of the Mind* during this trek, I believe I might have attempted to hike to Base Camp this morning. However, the book was full of stories about climbers who went too far when they should have turned back and ended up dead. I believe I was given this book for a reason. The message was simple. Know your body. Know your capabilities. Be honest with your assessment, even if it's incredibly difficult to do so.

So, all in all, I'm satisfied with my decision. I don't know if I'll ultimately have any regrets. Only time will tell. For now, I am at peace, and I am indebted to Karyn and Rich for buying me the book.

Two Sherpas led us down the mountain. The first was Pasang, a real gentleman. The other was Dawa, Pemba's brother. Dawa was the one who helped carry my backpack a few days ago when I was sick. Pemba, our sirdar, or leader of the Sherpas, is the brother-in-law of Tseten, the trekking company General Manager in Kathmandu. As I mentioned earlier, it helps to be related to someone or know someone who knows someone in order to be a Sherpa.

It took us almost four hours to get down to Pheriche. The first hour was a killer. My face was almost frostbitten. The wind was vicious. Every few minutes, I would remove my gloves from my hands in order to apply a bit of warmth to my nose and cheeks, from the palms of my semi-warm hands. The slightest bit of warmth was welcome. I couldn't keep my hands uncovered for very long, however, since my fingers would turn numb. This became a ritual during what seemed like an eternity. Fortunately, we were descending, so our hearts weren't working like locomotive pistons, as they had almost every day the previous week.

I paid no attention to the views the first hour. The stinging cold was way too mind numbing for me to think at all. The second hour, however, seemed almost effortless as the treacherous weather subsided, and we were able to take in more oxygen as we descended even farther. It was during this time that I couldn't help but think about what the rest of the team was going through on their way to Base Camp. They had to be hurting.

We hiked a long way, covering close to ten miles, first passing Lobuche and finally stopping to have lunch at the only teashop in Dzugla. I ate pan-fried macaroni and cheese with onions. Admittedly, I was starving since I hadn't eaten much in over a week, but it was fantastic. I thought about how much my older daughters would have loved the mac 'n cheese, but how the younger one would have turned up her nose at the onions.

My mind was already beginning to drift toward a happier, safer place, with my loved ones, now that I had reached the summit. Instead of constant worries, I was having more positive thoughts, knowing I was working my way down the mountain and ultimately back home. My pessimism was turning to optimism.

After lunch, the hike became even more manageable. The winds were gone, the sun was breaking through the clouds, and the temperature rose enough to make the trekking quite bearable. We moved hastily down the trail, feeling comfortable and well-fed. We were itching to get to Pheriche. We were hiking through the capacious Khumbu Valley, on a broad, slightly downward-sloping path, nestled between tall peaks in the distance on each side of us. We were still above the tree line, so there was little vegetation. Mostly, there were just wide-open rock and gravel fields and tiny streams flowing down the hills from higher up the valley.

While we were trekking, and with my heart not racing and pounding like a jack hammer as it had every other day on the ascent, I was finally able to have a conversation with Teddy and Mitch. The two of them have been glued at the hip for much of the trek, which is understandable since they are good friends from home. As a result, I never really got to know them well. We were joking that it was odd that we were first getting to know each other at this late stage of the trek, but we acknowledged that prior to that moment, there were numerous reasons why this had not been the case. At one point or another during the entire trek, we were all either too ill to want to have a conversation, too physically tired to speak as we were ascending, or too frozen and tired during most of the meals.

Teddy is a captain on a charter boat, and Mitch owns a small business. Both men are married and have been friends for years. They typically take a trip together every year, to do some male bonding. I told them I had wanted to do the same thing with my closest friends, but none of them were interested in trekking. And of course, our young kids made it even more complicated in terms of being able to get away. Teddy and Mitch both have kids, but a couple of them are in college and the others are already out of college and working. They therefore have no problems travelling whenever they feel like doing so.

Mitch has consistently maintained a blithe spirit. He has hated this trip as much as anyone, but he takes every single moment with a positive attitude, counteracting the despair by taking pictures with a very expensive camera he brought along. Teddy on the other hand, as nice a guy as he was, just couldn't wait to get the hell off the mountain. He wasn't holding back at all in expressing his unhappiness with the entire trek. It was interesting how the two of them complemented each other so well, with their different temperaments.

As we discussed the trek in great detail, they confirmed my suspicions that they had struggled as much as I had the past week. They both became very ill with dysentery, and admitted that they had totally underestimated the physical challenge. They were both taking Diamox all week, which they believe has helped them with the altitude – but there was no way to know for sure. They didn't have the paralyzing headaches I did, so I believe the Diamox must have helped them to some degree. We talked on and off for a couple of hours, even though it was painful for me to do so, with my throat still bothering me – but it helped pass the time and provided some normality to the situation. I hadn't had a two-hour conversation with anyone, even if it was somewhat intermittent, for a couple of weeks.

I also had a chance to speak with both Dawa and Pasang today. Pasang barely spoke English, so it was mainly me asking the questions and him answering "yes" or "no." Most of the time, he said, "yes," even though I had the feeling that he had no idea what I was talking about frequently. My conversation with Dawa was more engaging and informative. He gave me a solid understanding of how he and most other Sherpas aspire to do what they do, and explained that being a Sherpa is the only thing that he has wanted to do since he was a young boy. He told me he is 22 years old, but I don't believe it. He looks like a teenager. His goal is to be a Sherpa for many more years, in order to make enough money eventually to start some sort of business in the future – although he had no idea yet as to what kind of business. He said some of the Sherpas eventually start their own trekking businesses, basically as guides for hire, for trekkers who come to Nepal without a trekking company and then realize they need someone to guide them up the mountain, help with translation, room and board, etc. He used to be a porter and said he hated it and that it was a really tough job. No kidding.

I also asked him what he thought of Americans, and foreigners in general, who come to the Himalayas with all of their fancy gear and money, while Nepal has one of the lowest per capita incomes in the world. He said that most Americans were very good people and he loved his job and helping people on the mountain, adding that there weren't many opportunities for his people other than what he was doing. He also said that sometimes he meets people that are rude, but he doesn't care and it is his job to help them, no matter how they act.

The Sherpas are acclimated to the altitude, since they live here year round. They are also somewhat immune to the bacteria, being born and raised here, so they luckily don't deal with nearly the stomach issues. Dawa has consistently been chipper. He moves and bounces from rock-to-rock with the agility of a mountain goat. He is always smiling and making jokes, although I can't always understand them with his accent. He has a delightful personality and is an extremely good-looking guy. He's basically a stud and he's well aware of it.

Kim has been spending much of her time hanging with Dawa over the past couple of days. She is very tall, probably close to six feet, and slender. I'm not attracted to her at all, but I'm pretty sure Dawa would love to get into her sleeping bag. I have no idea if Kim has the same goal, but it has been interesting watching the dynamics between the two of them.

Watching them, I was reminded me of my teenage days working as a cabana boy at the Concord Hotel in the Catskills. There were carloads of beautiful women from New York City and as far away as Ohio, at this expensive hotel. Many of my buddies tried their hardest to hook up with the women. I fortunately had my girlfriend with me, who was working at a nearby hotel, so I didn't have to play the same game of "cat and mouse" as they all did. It was a constant effort on their part to woo them. It just goes to show that even thousands of miles away, in a very different country and decades later, boys will be boys.

When we finally made it to Pheriche late in the afternoon, I felt a huge burden lift. It was even more of a relief, and a welcome surprise, to find out that we'd be sleeping inside a tea lodge tonight. I am excited at the prospect of sleeping in a bed, no matter how uncomfortable it may possibly be, after the rough night last night.

I'm shacking up with Fernando. He's a handsome, dark skinned guy with curly hair and is relatively fit, but he has a small beer belly. Come to think of it, a few of the guys on the trek have beer bellies also. It's surprising considering they are trekkers. Fernando has a very strong accent, is thirty years old, single, and successful. He is an investment banker back home in Spain. Even though he's well off, he has had a roommate each night of the trek and preferred to have one again. My preference is to be in a single room, especially since the room costs a whopping $1.50 a night, but I didn't want to insult him. So I agreed to double up with him. I thought it was a bit strange that he paid a fortune for the trek, but wouldn't spend an extra $1.50 for a single room for one night. Regardless, it wasn't like we were going to be crammed into a tent, so I figured it wasn't worth trying to convince him otherwise. I only hope he doesn't snore, since I could use a good night sleep tonight.

11:00 P.M.

The four of us who descended today bought the Sherpas and porters dinner tonight. I ate some good food. The menu was limited – rice and vegetables. So I ordered both. I finally felt good enough to start eating. Since last week, when I was seriously ill, I have barely had an appetite. At first it was related to my nausea, but then I think it was the altitude. I'm sure I've lost at least ten pounds of body weight so far, if not more. I've never lost ten pounds in my life. When I think about the past ten days or so since arriving into Nepal, I have hardly had any protein in my diet. It's no wonder I've lost so much body mass so quickly.

After dinner, I gave Pasang a pair of my hiking boots. I also gave the porters my parka and some of my clothes, since I'm expecting it to get warmer as we descend. They were ecstatic to receive the gear and couldn't thank me enough. I felt it was the least I could do after what they've done for me.

What the Travel Brochure should have said:

Day 14: EVEREST BASE CAMP (OR NOT) • 17,575 feet

We will continue our trek with a visit to Everest Base Camp, with views of the icefall, unless you choose not to go. If you do go, expect the possibility of brutally cold weather, gale force winds, and hazardous conditions. Your body will be weak. Your headaches will be debilitating. Your ability to think rationally will be limited by the effects of altitude. The choice is yours. Think hard and think carefully. If you do not go to Base Camp, you will proceed down the valley into Pheriche. You will quickly start to feel better at the lower altitude, enabling you to think rationally and breathe easier.

12

THE EVEREST DIET

"We should not judge people by their peak of excellence; but by the distance they have traveled from the point where they started."

-Henry Ward Beecher

11-21-04

TRAVEL BROCHURE DESCRIPTION:

Day 15: PHERICHE • 13,950 feet

We head down the glacier and re-enter the lush and beautiful valleys, surrounded by spectacular snow-capped peaks. Upon reaching the village of Pheriche we will visit the Himalayan Rescue Association's Trekker's Aid Post.

Trekking Company Menu:

Wakeup tea / Coffee / Hot Chocolates

B/F:
Hash Brown Potato, Omlet, Porridge,
Tea / Coffee / Chocolates

Lunch:
Juice, Ham Burger, Salad, Brown Chips
Tea / Coffee / Chocolate

Refreshment
Tea / Coffee / Chocolates with Biscuits and snacks

Dinner:
Soup, Plain Pasta, Tomato Sausage, Toast Potato, Boil vegetables
Tea / Coffee / Chocolates

5:15 P.M.

I had an amazingly solid night's sleep last night, the first in ages and one that was long overdue. Fernando did, in fact, snore. At first, I thought it was going to be another difficult night. Luckily, he either stopped snoring quickly or I fell asleep instantaneously and simply didn't hear him because my body went into a self-induced coma.

Each of us who came down early ended up spending $18 in total for the room, three meals, treating the porters and Sherpas to their three meals as well, and for a "double" hot shower. A "double" shower requires the owner of the tea shop to climb on top of the shower shack twice, in order to fill the bucket both times with boiling water. This was quite a treat. I didn't want to have to rush like I did the other day. I should have ordered ten buckets.

The double shower also ended up being double the cost of my room. At this altitude, real estate is easy to come by, but fuel is not. The shower, of course, was outdoors and it was twenty-five degrees. Once the water stopped flowing, the cold air on my wet body acted like an external defibrillator, sending an electrical surge through my body and zapping me back to life.

Getting ready for a hot shower in Pheriche – with the bucket on top. The owner boils the water and pours it in the bucket and then the patron pulls a latch to release the water.

For the first time since arriving at Phadking over ten days ago, it felt great to be alive. I was feeling stronger and was able to think more clearly. I was finally well-rested from a good night's sleep. I had eaten a couple of edible meals. The lower altitude allowed me to take in much more oxygen and breathe easier. I was actually enjoying myself for the very first time this entire trip, being in the Himalayas and taking in the views without feeling awful. Even my headache was gone.

I am still taking the Cipro, which has been keeping any stomach bugs at bay. I don't know if it is doing any damage to my body in the process, but I'm willing to take the risk in order to prevent getting dysentery again and living through another night of horror as I did in Dingboche.

We sat around for a couple of hours, waiting for the rest of the team to arrive from Gorak Shep. It was a wonderfully sunny day. Pheriche, at approximately 14,000 feet, is a sizable town considering the high altitude. There were a few dozen homes and teashops. We strolled around for a while, enjoying the fresh air, the beautiful views, and the crisp weather. It was cold, but it felt comfortable with the sun shining brightly. It was also a pleasure being able to stroll casually through the town without a backpack and without having to hike to a particular destination, especially one much higher up the mountain.

Pheriche is the base for the Himalayan Rescue Association. As I entered their building, I immediately noticed a gorgeous, young blonde female doctor with dazzlingly blue eyes sitting at her desk. She gave me a great big warm smile, which lit up my heart. She started saying hello to me, but it took me a few seconds to hear what she was saying because she was so damn beautiful. If Donna was a "10," Dr. Gorgeous was a "20." I came back to my senses and had a brief conversation with her, starting with "Wow, you're just what the doctor ordered." That got me an even bigger smile, although she was probably thinking to herself, "Is that the best line you have?"

She was Canadian and had been doing a rotation here for two full months and was now eager to go home. She said it was a great experience, but she was sick of the cold weather. And she's from Canada! I didn't feel too bad for her, considering the tiny clinic seemed like it offered more creature comforts than most places at 14,000 feet, at least more than all of those I had visited. Even though I didn't ask, I bet she even had a toilet with a seat in her bathroom.

During her short tenure there, she primarily helped people with altitude and gastro-intestinal problems. No surprise there. I wanted to continue talking to her about anything and everything, but eventually, I was at a loss for words.

I purchased a couple of T-shirts at the clinic to support the Rescue Center. While there, I noticed there was a scale in the room, so I decided to weigh myself. I stood on it with my clothes on, but I took off my hiking boots and jacket. When I looked down at the scale, I immediately assumed it was broken. I asked Dr. Gorgeous if it was in fact not working and she assured me it was "deadly accurate." It was an interesting choice of words. Regardless, I was blown away to see my body weight down to 150 pounds, net of a couple of pounds for the weight of my clothes. I have weighed 165 pounds, almost consistently, for the past ten years – unable to lose or gain much weight during that entire time span. It was hard to believe I have lost fifteen pounds. When I mentioned it to the other guys, they couldn't believe it.

Dr. Gorgeous overheard the conversation and mentioned to me I was probably losing weight because of the cold weather. She told me my body was losing weight constantly simply by being cold every day. Apparently, the more I had shivered during this trek, the more energy I was using and it was causing a constant loss of calories. I didn't have the heart to tell her I lost the weight because I had dysentery for a few days and I hadn't eaten much food in more than a week, in addition to exercising harder than I ever had for six to seven hours almost every day.

Afterward, while sitting around with the guys waiting for the rest of our team to arrive, I thought of a brand new diet – the Everest Diet – or maybe the Everest Base Camp Diet. I rejected the Kala Patthar Diet; it didn't sound very catchy.

Want to lose 15 pounds in 10 days? All you have to do is trek in the Himalayas. You don't even have to climb to the top of Everest, or even go to Base Camp. All you have to do is be in the vicinity of this place and you are basically guaranteed to lose weight through the simple means of nausea, loss of appetite, dysentery, and constant shivering. Want to lose 50 pounds? Stay for a month – take an extended vacation – just make sure you stay alive in the process.

The rest of the group finally started arriving, one by one, from Gorak Shep. Jack and Ian arrived first, of course. We were anxious to find out how the previous day had gone. They informed us the weather continued to be intolerable. This was no surprise, based on the weather we had experienced on the way down to Pheriche yesterday morning. The weather at Gorak Shep and Base Camp must have been punishing. Jack said Randy had turned back almost immediately after starting out for Base Camp. Randy has barely said a word the entire trek. He has struggled most of the time, more than the rest of us if you could believe it, but he is a determined son-of-a-bitch. I admire him for his valiant effort. Even though he didn't make it, at least he tried. I don't know if it was smart, but it was certainly bold.

Shortly after Randy turned back, three others – Robin, Kim, and Bruce – also gave up as well, concerned about the extreme conditions and their safety. So out of the twelve of us in the group, besides the guides, only four people made it to Base Camp...Jack, Ian, Jay and George. I knew the "fast guys" would make it. I wouldn't have expected anything less. They are machines. I was happy for George that he made it as well. He hasn't moved fast this entire trek, but he has also never complained. He just kept pushing on.

We of course asked them what we missed at Base Camp, and they informed us we didn't miss anything at all. They told us besides the Khumbu Icefall, which was in fact "cool," there wasn't anything else to see. The rest of the group eventually arrived two hours after Jack and Ian. They looked absolutely awful.

As much as I regretted not seeing the Khumbu Icefall, I'm glad I made the decision not to go. The four of us who came down yesterday were well-rested for the additional five miles we hiked earlier today. This trek is still not finished, by any means. We need to get back down safely.

Our itinerary had called for us to originally stay in Pheriche tonight, but Lorraine wanted us to move on to the next town, Pangboche, since we had a significant amount of distance to cover in only a couple of days in order to get back to Lukla. The hike to Pangboche, at 13,100 feet, was uneventful and took us about two hours. It's amazing how much ground one can cover when gravity is helping out.

10:30 P.M., Town of Pangboche

Although we were supposed to stay in a tent tonight, we ended up at a tea lodge which didn't have room for tents on their grounds. My room is decorated, if you could call it that, in 70's hippie style. The bedspreads are psychedelic, and they are filthy. I put my sleeping bag on top of the bedspread, since I don't know what creatures – bedbugs or worse – are actually nesting there. I can't even imagine how many unwashed bodies, like mine prior to my shower yesterday, have slept on the bedspread over the many years since it was last washed.

Although it is a cool twenty-three degrees inside of my room now, I have taken off my down vest. My body is becoming slightly immune to the cold. I may be turning into a cold-blooded mammal. All kidding aside, since I am feeling better, I feel less cold, even though the temperature hasn't changed much. It is one less layer for me and, more important, another step closer to being home.

I turned the page of my journal and found this letter from Lexie, my 9-year-old daughter:

Dear Daddy,
          I hope that you
are happy at Mt. Everest.
I hope you are having a
great time. I miss you alot
and are very happy that you
made a dream come true. I
hope you are having the
funnest time of your life
Make sure that everything
you wanted to do, happens
I will be very happy if you
see this page. Remember that
I will always love you. I will
always hope that your hopes
will come true. Make sure you
meet alot of people in your
group. I know it was one
of your dreams to climb
mount Everest, and guess
what you're already climbing
19,000 feet. I hope you
have a great time and
meet new people and
have a safe trip/flight
                    — Lexie Schachne

Thanks Lexie. This certainly isn't the "funnest" trip ever, but you just made it slightly more enjoyable. I love you.

What the Travel Brochure should have said:

Day 15: PANGBOCHE • 13,950 feet

We head down the glacier and re-enter the lush and beautiful valleys, surrounded by spectacular snow-capped peaks. After pure anguish for the past ten days, you will finally start feeling better after descending from higher altitude. With your bodily functions operating at a higher capacity, you should begin to feel like your old self. Upon reaching the village of Pheriche, you will visit the Himalayan Rescue Association Trekker Aid Post, where a beautiful doctor will be filling in for two months. She will be a wonderful sight for sore eyes. If you are going to be sick on the mountain, there isn't a better day than today for a house call.

13

SOLITUDE

"Settle yourself in solitude, and you will come upon God in yourself."

-Teresa de Avila

11-22-04

TRAVEL BROCHURE DESCRIPTION:

Day 16: NAMCHE BAZAAR • 11,300 feet

Today we trek back along the Dudh Kosi River through a magnificent rhododendron forest and past brilliant waterfalls. Shortly before reaching Namche, the trek takes us through a pine forest, where musk deer often graze in the early morning. Arriving in town, we may see lowland porters, highland Sherpas, and Tibetan people trading food and supplies during Namche's market time.

Trekking Company Menu:

Wakeup tea / Coffee / Hot Chocolates

B/F:
Rice Porridge, Boil eggs, Cramp Pan Cake
Tea / Coffee / Chocolates

Lunch:
Juice, Tibetan Bread, Mixed Salad, Tuna Fish, Potato Sote
Tea / Coffee / Chocolate

Refreshment
Tea / Coffee / Chocolates with Biscuits and snacks

Dinner:
Soup, Spaghetti with Bollenice, Sausage, Yak Steak,
Boiled Beans, Cauliflower
Tea / Coffee/ Chocolates

Early evening, Namche Bazaar

I heard some gossip on the hike today. A few of the guys were speaking to each other and mentioned they heard "female sounds of pleasure" coming from one of the rooms last night. The walls were paper thin. They all think it was Kim. As I mentioned the other day, she has been spending a great deal of time around Dawa. There have been consistent rumors swirling around of some hanky-panky going on between them. Yet, although it sounded like moans of pleasure to the guys, it's certainly possible it could have been someone with intense stomach cramps. Even if it was a couple of people enjoying each other, I have no way of knowing if it was in fact Dawa and Kim, or possibly Bruce and Dakotah, or even Lorraine and someone else. For all I know it could have been the teashop owner and her husband.

Most of the guys believed it was Dawa and Kim, since they were together the entire day yesterday on the hike to Pheriche and Pangboche. Regardless, anything is possible. If something did happen between Kim and Dawa, or anyone else for that matter, then good for them as long as they both were willing participants. I would think this kind of hookup goes on frequently in an environment like this. Anyway, I have bigger concerns on my mind.

We started the day at 6:00 AM since we had lots of ground to cover, probably over ten miles. We ate the standard lousy breakfast. I can't wait to get back home and have scrambled eggs with melted cheese, or banana pancakes with Vermont maple syrup or even my favorite, Skippy peanut butter and Smucker's jam on Wonder Bread. Yummy.

We began hiking at around 8:00 A.M. We had a long way to go before lunch. Instead of backtracking on the same path we had travelled on the way up the mountain, past the monastery, we took a different trail toward Namche Bazaar, on the opposite side of the river and across the valley. Lorraine suggested taking this route, informing us it was harder and longer, but much more scenic.

I decided to start out by walking with the "fast guys," but it was wishful thinking on my part that I could possibly keep pace with them for very long. While I was trying to stay in step with them, I thought about the expression I've heard time and time again; "Life is about the journey, not the destination." Over the years, I've tried to keep this in mind, sometimes living by it but, frequently, forgetting it. It seemed truly crazy that the "fast guys" goal every single day was simply getting to the next destination and not enjoying the journey itself, or so it seemed. I don't think they ever even stopped for a quick view, although I wouldn't know since I didn't keep pace with them.

To some degree, I guess I couldn't blame them for rushing on the way up to Kala Patthar the past week, since hiking into higher altitudes just plain sucked. They wanted to get to the next campsite as quickly as possible, minimize the pain, and have a drink or two (or three) – in order to drown out their sorrows. It was hard work and it was tiring, so why not rush if they could physically pull it off? However, on the way down, it is a very different story...or at least I believe so. Why the need to hurry? Maybe they viewed it as a physical contest or a test of manliness more than anything else.

I kept up with them for about a half-hour, but they eventually left me in the dust. Maybe I was cramping their style. I really didn't care since I was feeling good and enjoying myself. I decided to take a break to snap some pictures, which, incredibly to me, is something I haven't really done much this entire trek. I say "incredibly" because I used to love photography and at one point early in my life I thought about becoming a photographer. Unfortunately, up until yesterday, I was in no mood to take pictures each day as I dealt with all of my hardships. I think I have taken fewer than a hundred pictures here so far, versus the thousand or more I had expected to take.

During the break, I had a drink of water, ate a snack, took some pictures, and enjoyed the marvelous scenery. What I thought would take only a few minutes ended up taking twenty minutes or more. It was the first time on this trek I just took in the views and didn't feel terribly ill. As a matter of fact, I felt great. It was wonderful to feel as if I was finally in control of my own destiny. For once, the mountains were mine. I was in awe of the views and I was shocked that not a single soul had strolled by during the entire time.

When I finally put my backpack on and started hiking again, there still wasn't a human, or a yak, in sight. The rest of the group still hadn't caught up with me. This alone should give you a good indication of how fast the "fast guys" and I were walking earlier. And speaking of the "fast guys," they were long gone – nowhere in view on the wide open mountain.

For the next two hours, I hiked alone and experienced total solitude, as I never have before. I've hiked in many different places around the world. In every case, I was always in sight of another person on the trail. Not today. I had the valley completely to myself. It was (almost) impossible to get lost since there was only one trail, so I felt safe and secure. I was high, literally and figuratively, with no headaches, stomach pains, or dysentery. And for the first time on the trek, I wasn't even coughing. It was the closest thing to heaven on earth.

I hiked along the trail for miles. I was on the opposite side of the valley from where we had ascended days earlier and I could see the beautiful Tengboche monastery off in the distance. Otherwise, there was no sign of civilization at all.

I was completely in the moment. The weather, although cool, was perfect for hiking. It was a splendidly sunny day. The trail was mostly packed dirt, instead of embedded and loose rocks, so I was able to take in some of the views as I was walking without the constant fear of tripping. Since I didn't have to stare at the ground the entire time, I didn't have a tension-headache or sore neck. It was great to feel healthy and to finally be able to enjoy my surroundings.

The scenery was stunning, just as Lorraine had promised. I could see for miles and miles across the valley, yet I still couldn't see anyone on the trail. There were a few moments when I had some concerns that I possibly had taken a wrong turn somewhere, but I was relatively confident I hadn't. So I kept moving along, assuming things were fine. After so many problems during this trip, anything was possible – but for the first time, I wasn't worried.

The air was fresh and pure. There weren't any yaks from our group, or any other group, kicking up dust. Fortunately for me, and also for the yaks, they had taken the shorter path to Namche Bazaar. There was also no sign at all of burning yak dung, or even a trace of the odor of it, since there were no teashops or tea lodges in sight. I was thinking I wouldn't be breathing clean air like this once I arrived back into New York, so I was sucking it all in. I had been starving for oxygen the past few days and accordingly, had a voracious appetite for it.

Hiking from Pangboche to Namche Bazaar across the river from Tengboche Monastery, in complete solitude.

Near the end of the first three hours of hiking, I passed through an area of lush green farms. The first thing I thought of when I saw the town was the remake of the movie *Lost Horizon*. I hadn't thought much about this movie in almost thirty years. It was bizarre that this was the first thing that popped into my mind, and even more so considering I hadn't thought of the movie earlier in the trek, when I had been hiking up to Kala Patthar all week. I had passed similarly green fields during that time, but of course, I wasn't feeling well. Now, I was feeling great and, wham, "Shangri-La" appeared in my thoughts.

The movie Lost Horizon premiered in 1973, when I was 12 years old – a few months prior to attending summer camp. I hadn't been exposed to the outdoors, yet.

I remember the movie vividly to this day. It opens up with a small plane from China crashing in the Himalayas. The surviving passengers arduously trek through a blizzard, fighting brutally harsh winds, and dragging themselves through deep snow, until they arrive at "the Valley of the Blue Moon," otherwise known as "Shangri-La." In this isolated land of "Shangri-La," completely closed off from the outside world, there is no snow, no cold and no hatred – only marvelous green hills and mountains, flowing waterfalls, fertile land, and racial harmony – heaven on earth. An imaginary paradise.

I was captivated by the story, the beautiful scenery, moving music and the concept of "eternal youth."

The movie is based on a 1933 novel by the same name, written by James Hilton, who also wrote *Goodbye Mr. Chips*. *Lost Horizon* was published after World War I, after the crash on Wall Street in 1929, and a few years after the start of the Great Depression. Hilton created "Shangri-La" as a mythical Himalayan utopia.

The more I researched the theme of the movie, years after my trek, the more I started to understand the role it had played in my life. I believe it helped me perceive "nature" in general, and the Himalayas in particular, as a place for me to escape some of the ugliness I experienced as a youth, particularly the fighting and the ethnic hatred I encountered in my Brooklyn neighborhood – and it occurred at just around the time I was preparing to attend summer camp in the Catskills. I don't believe it was the movie in and of itself that molded me. Still, the idea of such a place exerted a powerful attraction for me. I finally started to comprehend why I had had a burning desire, for so long, to be in the Himalayas.

Although I acknowledged earlier that no place is perfect, I clearly didn't think that way when I was a kid. I had thus pegged, in my mind, the Himalayas as my "Shangri-La."

The town I passed through today, Phortse, wasn't green and lush, with flowing waterfalls, as in the movie, but it was otherwise a beautiful, serene setting, in the middle of the frigid Himalayas. It amazed me that a two-day hike from Everest Base Camp, a place existed where people appeared to be living comfortable, happy lives and growing abundant crops. Locals were out and about, doing their chores. I was enjoying myself more and more with each passing moment, and began to question when it was all going to end. It didn't take long.

A farming town, Phortse, at approximately 14,000 feet.

Immediately after reaching the town, I joined up with the "fast guys" who were waiting there for the rest of the team to arrive. We waited another half hour or so before everyone else finally joined us. We then had to cross the river to get back to the other side of the valley, so we could reach Namche Bazaar. We thus had to hike down seven hundred feet to the river, which was obviously very easy and refreshing. Unfortunately, we then had to hike up one thousand feet to get back on the proper trail, in order to head back into Namche Bazaar.

This would have been par for the course on the way up to Kala Patthar a few days ago, but things were different now, or at least we expected them to be. Everyone except for Fernando had reached the summit. We had all put in the hard work already. We had paid our dues. We thought or, rather foolishly, assumed, it would be smooth sailing from here on in. We were mistaken.

The thousand foot hike up from the river was an absolute killer – more challenging than any other day, except for the day we reached the summit of Kala Patthar – or maybe it just seemed this way since our bodies were basically lifeless. Regardless, the climb was brutally steep, with countless tiny, tortuous switchbacks most of the way up. It was as if were climbing multiple tall skyscrapers for a couple of hours.

Everyone was angry. After all they had been through on this trek, they felt cheated. "If there was a much shorter and easier route, going the original way we came up the valley, why didn't you send us that way?" they were shouting at Lorraine, while struggling to catch their breath, as if they were on life support.

At lunch, my fellow trekkers acted like an angry mob, out to lynch Lorraine. Some members of the team were fuming mad, with indignant expressions plastered on their faces. This was highly unusual, since the entire group had co-existed extremely well the past two weeks. There were minimal complaints or confrontations the entire time. And if there were, we always worked them out amicably.

Most everyone acknowledged they made an awful decision choosing to go on this trek in the first place, but they felt it was an extremely misguided decision on Lorraine's part to suggest taking the path we took today. I was startled by how a few of the guys became unhinged, especially Teddy and Mitch, since I hadn't seen this side of them before. A few others were just as angry, but voiced their anger indirectly amongst the team versus with Lorraine directly. Either way, she definitely got the message.

As much as I was shocked by their reactions, I understood why they were so livid. People were still not feeling well, just as I had not felt well at all up until yesterday. They didn't have any desire, in essence, to climb another Kala Patthar two days after the first.

If I was as sick as I had been a few days ago, I'm sure I would have been furious and joined the lynching party. Luckily for me, I was feeling great. And the more I thought about it, the more I believed Lorraine had made the right decision. It was a backbreaking climb, but it was still the most enjoyable day of the entire trek for me since I wasn't ill, and I was therefore able to endure it just fine.

Don't get me wrong, it was a bitch to climb and I was cursing Lorraine under my breath as I was doing it. However, thinking back, it was a good decision taking us on a different path from those we had travelled previously. It is unlikely any of us will be returning to the Himalayas, especially any time soon, so why not see something new, especially when what we were seeing was so beautiful and majestic?

I felt sorry for Lorraine since she thought she was doing the right thing. I don't think she fully realized the horrible condition everyone is in. People are hurting. We are all thoroughly depleted. Nobody wants to be here anymore. I think it simply didn't register with her, since she has completed this trek so many times and has become immune to the physical and mental challenges – unlike the rest of us.

Ultimately, we connected with the original trail we had taken on the way up to Tengboche and spent about two hours walking down the path back to Namche Bazaar. Fortunately, everyone's tempers had cooled down once we started trekking again. There was no time or energy to remain outraged. Unfortunately, we were stuck behind a dozen yaks the entire way down and ended up ingesting clouds of dust, which the yaks kicked up as they took each stride, supporting their monstrous bodies. I tried no less than ten times to pass them. Each time, I came close to being gored. As anxious as I was to get down, I finally decided to listen to Lorraine's advice, which she had given to us at the start of the trek, to not attempt to pass the yaks. So after an hour of trying, I finally relented and decided to play it safe. I had survived until now. I realized it wasn't worth doing something stupid and getting injured with only two days to go. I waited for a few minutes until the yaks were a hundred yards or so ahead of me, so that the dust dissipated, and then followed them, slowly, the entire way into town.

I arrived at Namche Bazaar at 3:30 P.M. The first thing I did was drop off my gear and then immediately rush to my favorite pizza joint. I had the most heavenly, gooey, cheesy hot pizza ever. It felt so good to have real food in my stomach. I could have eaten ten pies. If only they could have delivered pizzas to all of the teashops I stayed at on the way up to Kala Patthar. What a different trek it would have been!

Afterward, around 6 P.M., I went to the Internet cafe to get on "Instant Messenger" with Faith and the girls. It was morning back home. After we connected online, I was so excited that I decided to call them as well. We spoke for a couple of minutes even though I knew it was going to bankrupt me, and even though I could barely speak because of some unknown problem with my throat. I had had a sore throat for two weeks, but there was something else going on with it that I couldn't figure out. In any case, it was great hearing their voices and speaking with them. It gave me an incredible feeling of joy, unlike I had experienced since leaving home. I never thought I could miss them all as much as I did. I longed to be back together with them, to hug, laugh, and play with them.

After I made the phone call, I walked around town for a while, taking in the sights. Namche Bazaar was bustling as usual.

I watched a few trekkers negotiate some deals with shop owners. The trekkers going up the mountain were buying hiking gear and those coming down the mountain were selling their gear and buying souvenirs. They were getting ready to go home and see their families, just like me. I looked around for gifts for the girls for quite a while. There were hundreds of items to choose from but hardly anything I thought they would actually want. I purchased a couple of hats and some small Nepalese-designed pill boxes. They have multi-colored pieces of plastic looking like gem stones. I'm sure the girls will think they are real rubies and diamonds. Or at least I'll tell them so.

The streets and shops of Namche Bazaar.

11:00 P.M. Namche Bazaar

The lodge we are staying at tonight is supposedly the newest and nicest place in town. Although it doesn't come close to the pure luxury of a Motel 6, it still seems like a palace to me, compared to what I have experienced the past two weeks. My room has a real bathroom with a flushing toilet...and even a shower. I can't believe it actually has a toilet with a seat. I can't wait to take a crap. I'm not sure why Lorraine didn't have us stay here on the way up to Kala Patthar when we passed through Namche last week, but I'm not complaining.

The room is barren, with just a bed and a chair, but there are freshly painted gray walls. Unfortunately, I couldn't use the shower earlier since the water is heated by solar power. It was dark outside by the time I got back to my room and all of the hot water had been used up. I found this out the cold, hard way. So I took a shower in another part of the building where the water was boiled from yak dung. It felt great to be in a real shower, inside of a real building, and not outside in the cold. I didn't even mind the burning, smoky yak dung – well, I did, but I was willing to put up with it because I was in a much better frame of mind.

Tomorrow is the last hiking day and it's going to be a very long one. Girls, I love you and I can't wait to see you.

What the Travel Brochure should have said:

Day 16: NAMCHE BAZAAR • 11,300 feet

Today we take a different path back to Namche Bazaar. If you're feeling well, it will be a wonderful experience. However, we're going to throw you a curve ball in the late morning, testing your endurance. We promised you an adventure, didn't we? You'll continue to feel better as you descend. You can say goodbye to your headaches, and if you're lucky, your stomach cramps. You'll head back to Namche Bazaar and pig out on a hot pizza. It will taste better than anything you've ever eaten.

14

OXYGEN

"It is good to have an end to journey toward, but it is the journey that matters in the end."

- Oddly, both Ursula K. Le Guin and Ernest Hemingway are credited for coining this phrase.

11-23-04

TRAVEL BROCHURE DESCRIPTION:

Day 17: LUKLA • 9,350 feet

Trek from Namche Bazaar to Lukla where we will spend the night.

Menu:

Wakeup tea / Coffee / Hot Chocolates

B/F:
Toast Bread, Porridge, Omlet
Tea / Coffee / Chocolates

Lunch:
Juice, Puri, Potato Salad, Meat, Beans
Tea / Coffee / Chocolate

Refreshment
Tea / Coffee / Chocolates with Biscuits and snacks

Dinner:
Soup, Fried Macaroni, Tomato Sausage, Potato Bread,
Vegetable Boiled, Desert
Tea / Coffee/ Chocolates

Late Evening, back in Lukla

I opened my hotel room door this morning and saw all of Namche Bazaar covered with a fresh coating of snow. It was still snowing, with close to three inches on the ground, when we started hiking. Even so, it turned out to be a great day. We had a wonderful hike down to Lukla. Although the sun never came out, it stopped snowing by late morning. I decided to skip lunch, since I knew I wouldn't be missing very much. I ended up hiking with the "fast guys" – all three of them. Amazingly, I kept up with them the entire way down. We hiked for almost six hours without stopping, straight through to Lukla. Yes, I know....it's all about the journey, yadda, yadda, yadda. Well, screw it. I felt great and wanted to finish the trek and get the heck off the trail. I had had enough of trekking for a very long time. During the entire six hours, nobody said a word to anyone. I finally got to see the "fast guys" in all of their glory. It was "no talk and all action."

My lungs were in perfect working condition the entire the day, feeling as if I was in an oxygen bar and drinks were on the house. I was high on thick air. The lower I descended, the higher I became. The thermometer hit forty degrees in the middle of the afternoon. Life was good. The very last mile of the trek was uphill, but it was an easy walk since the air was so much thicker at 9,000 feet. I felt as strong as a yak or a porter, and as fast and nimble as a Sherpa.

The only unfortunate thing was that since it was getting warmer at the lower altitude, it was very buggy. The mosquitoes can't survive the cool temperatures higher up in the hills, but they were living a very happy life down here, and they were trying to eat me alive.

We were moving at lightning speed the whole time, dodging Sherpas, porters, yaks, and locals. We had to be light and fast on our feet, in order to avoid the rivers of feces. The snow, which had fallen earlier in the morning, was melting throughout the day and mixing with the yak dung on the trails, in turn causing it to flow down the trails. The trails were filled with waste everywhere, because the path from Namche to Lukla is well-traveled – and well-trampled. And when the yaks gotta go, they go. And they go big – think horse, hippo or rhino big. It was difficult distinguishing the yak dung from the mud. Both were everywhere, mixed together into a thick chocolate shake. And with all of the snow melting, it was flowing like the Hudson River. There were even little mud (and shit) falls, instead of waterfalls, gushing down from one part of the trail to the next.

The scariest moments were when we were walking downhill on the very steep parts of the trail. Gravity was causing us to move at a very rapid pace. I came very close to slipping in shit many times. I was waiting for it to happen, since it would have been a perfect ending to the perfect storm this trek has been.

On a more positive note, it was an amazing change of scenery heading down the mountain today – a metamorphosis in the landscapes – as we went from snowy Namche Bazaar with snow capped peaks far in the distance, to wooded trails and forest, where everything was a brilliant green. Farms became more and more frequent, and then teashops, and then the big town of Lukla, with all of its merchants...and finally, the airport. Civilization – Himalayan style.

Our dinner tonight was a Chinese meal; spicy chicken, chow mein, spring rolls, and fried rice. I skipped the chicken. I had done a good job of avoiding meat on the trek, except for the few slices of salami I had, which I'll regret eating for the rest of my life since I'll associate it forever with that awful night in Dingboche.

After dinner, the entire team of Sherpas, porters, and kitchen staff, approximately two dozen in all, came into the tea lodge. We gave them their tips, which they so richly deserved. These incredibly gracious people had all worked so hard for our well-being and comfort. I can't even imagine how much worse this trek would have been if they hadn't helped us through our darkest days. We bought them drinks and we danced with them to Nepalese music. We all had a wonderful time.

Six members of our group, led by the "fast guys," decided to celebrate by getting shit-faced tonight – not literally (although I guess anything is possible in this environment), just figuratively. The "fast guys" had started drinking once they arrived into town, as they had every other day, prior to the rest of the team arriving. The gang of six – Jack, Ian, Jay, Teddy, Mitch and Fernando – purchased more than fifty beers. They were completely drunk, more plastered than my college roommates ever were – and those guys knew how to party for hours on end. They piled the cans high on the table and created a huge mountain out of them – a visual metaphor – a Kala Patthar of beer cans. It was a tribute to our trek. And of course, they ceremoniously knocked them all down, as if to say, "We fucking did it and now we're getting the hell out of here."

Throughout the evening, I noticed that much of my gear, which I had given away to the staff, was being put to good use. One of the porters was wearing the hiking boots I gave him, another was wearing my long johns (as his pants), and yet another was wearing the expedition parka I had given him, inside of the heated tea lodge. They were ecstatic to have it all and wanted to show their appreciation by wearing it. It made me happy to know they would have some quality gear as they escorted future groups of unsuspecting trekkers up the mountain.

What the Travel Brochure should have said:

Day 17: LUKLA • 9,350 feet

Trek from Namche Bazaar to Lukla where we will spend the night. You will be thrilled and thankful knowing you will be heading home in a couple of days. Your nightmare is coming to an end – almost. You still need to get lucky flying back to Kathmandu safely. The odds are in your favor, but we make no guarantees. You will have some regrets leaving since you probably weren't capable of enjoying the beautiful mountains all around you until recently, but you really won't care. You just want to go home.

15

SORRY EYES

*"A journey, I reflected, is of no merit
unless it has tested you."*

-Tahir Shah

11-24-04

TRAVEL BROCHURE DESCRIPTION:

Day 18: KATHMANDU • 4,383 feet

If the weather is clear, the morning flight back to Kathmandu will be a scenic and smooth farewell to the mountains.

Trekking Company Menu:

Wakeup tea / Coffee / Hot Chocolates

B/F:
Corn-flakes, Pan Cake, Scramble egg
Tea / Coffee / Chocolates

Lunch:
Juice, Bon/Bread, Salad, Potato with steam, Cheese, Beans Boil
Tea / Coffee / Chocolate

Refreshment
Tea / Coffee / Chocolates with Biscuits and snacks

Dinner:
Soup, Nepalese Dish, Momo, Curry, Sausage, salad, Desert
Tea / Coffee / Chocolates

Late evening, Kathmandu

I couldn't sleep beyond 6 A.M. this morning. I was way too anxious about making my flight home. I got out of my bed in the tea lodge and walked up and down the one and only road (trail) stretching through Lukla's main commercial hub. The town was quiet, but it was starting to come alive, as in any city in the early morning. Some porters were already going up the mountain trying to get an early start, in order to beat the morning rush of trekkers, Sherpas, school children, and yaks.

When the shops finally opened around 8 A.M., I bought some candy and locally produced chewing gum to bring back home for my girls. Then I relaxed in the tea lodge while waiting for breakfast. We had planned to go to the airport for our flight from Lukla to Kathmandu around 10 A.M., but there aren't any officially scheduled flights. The planes basically arrive and depart whenever the weather cooperates. And in the mountains, the weather doesn't cooperate.

Ten o'clock came and went. Murphy's Law was at play again, as expected. There was bad weather in Kathmandu. Even though it was sunny in Lukla, the flights weren't taking off from Kathmandu to bring new trekkers here, and thus there were no planes available to take us to back to Kathmandu. It was extremely nerve-wracking waiting for the flight, considering we were all itching to go home. We had a perfect view of the runway from a window in the combined dining room/sitting area in the tea lodge.

Finally, after waiting for what seemed like an eternity, we saw the first plane arriving at 11:30 A.M. It was thrilling watching it land. The incoming plane has to fly down into the valley, way below the landing strip, and then ascend as it comes in for the landing. It's basically the opposite of what almost all other planes have to do to land elsewhere. As I mentioned at the beginning of the trek, there have been many plane crashes flying into and out of Lukla. Just the same, there aren't nearly as many as you'd expect, based on actually seeing what death-defying moves the pilots have to make in order to take off and land.

We continued to wait for another two hours. There was a backlog of trekkers who needed to be cleared out. Luckily, many more flights were arriving and departing. We were finally summoned to the airport at 1:30 P.M. We went through security, which was comical, since it took us all of three seconds to get through it, and then we waited in a small, barren holding room for almost another hour and a half. The wait at the airport was agonizing. I was desperate to get off the mountain and that much closer to home. To help fill the time, I tried to calculate how many steps I had taken the past couple of weeks. I figured it was close to three hundred thousand, give or take.

It's crazy to think that I had wanted to come here for more than two decades, but now I couldn't wait to go home after just two weeks.

As I was sitting there waiting for the flight, I realized this trek had been agonizingly difficult for almost everyone. It wasn't just those in our trekking group. I could see it in each pair of eyes of every exhausted, hungry, sickly-looking trekker, and in their every movement. It didn't matter who you were, how healthy you were, or how physically fit. Even the fastest of the "fast guys" – those fittest and manliest of men – still succumbed to the forces of nature, at one point or another.

We finally boarded the plane and took off minutes before the clouds started rolling in. If we had left five minutes later, we would have been stuck in Lukla for another day, and I would have missed my flights back home to the U.S.

We arrived at the hotel I had looked down at just two weeks ago, at around 4:00 P.M. It now seemed like the height of luxurious accommodations. I jumped into the shower in my room as fast as humanly possible. It felt exhilarating. I washed my hair a few times. I dried myself off and took a sniff of my skin. I was clean! I smelled good! I couldn't believe it. After all I had gone through, it was wonderful to be back in Kathmandu, the same big city I couldn't wait to get away from two weeks earlier. I opened the window and screamed, "I love you Kathmandu!" It killed my throat. I had forgotten for a second that parts of my body were still in bad shape.

Afterward, I went with George and Randy into Thamel, the main shopping area of Kathmandu. It was the first time on the entire trip that Randy had said more than a half-dozen words. He had come alive, as had I. It just took him a bit longer. Thamel is a mixture of New Orleans, Greenwich Village, some Haight Ashbury out of the 60's, and similar locales. It's a very hippy-ish part of town.

There were major traffic jams, with exhaust fumes turning the air gray, and hundreds of motorcycles, scooters and dirt bikes zipping in and out of the traffic with amazing agility. And there were hundreds of stores selling anything you could imagine, including the kitchen sink, along with tons of handcrafted items, and, of course, Tiger Balm. It was everywhere. Tiger Balm is basically a heat rub, but many people here believe it cures all sorts of maladies and has mysterious powers. It is made from a secret herbal formulation dating back to the times of the Chinese emperors. It is sold in the U.S., so I didn't "buy it."

We had to be very careful walking in Thamel since there are few sidewalks, and the vehicles weave in and out of the crowds of people. We were joking with each other that it was safer to be back in the Khumbu Valley than on the streets of Thamel. We spent a couple of hours walking around and were accosted by many of the street vendors.

I bought some tie-dyed T-shirts for the girls and a miniature handcrafted backgammon set and then we headed to dinner in Thamel at a place called Rum Doodle, an institution in Nepal. It is a restaurant/bar that has become a popular destination for trekkers and climbers from all over the world. Almost everyone who has reached the summit of Everest has received membership at Rum Doodle and a free meal. Each successful climber, and then some, has received (or purchased) a paper or wooden cutout of a giant footprint, that is affixed to the wall near the bar. Patrons sign a footprint and then attempt to find an empty spot for it anywhere in the restaurant, where it will be seen by other patrons for future generations – or until they run out of space and start over again. Teddy and Mitch bought one for the team and we all signed it. If you have ignored everything I have written thus far and you decide to go trekking in Nepal, go to Rum Doodle and you can look for my signature on the footprint from 11-24-2004.

A plane taking off and heading to Kathmandu.

What the Travel Brochure should have said:

Day 18: KATHMANDU • 4,383 feet

If the weather is clear, the morning flight back to Kathmandu will be a scenic and smooth farewell to the mountains. Don't count on it, however. As you've probably found out, the weather here is unpredictable. Keep your fingers crossed and your eyes closed.

CHAPTER FIFTEEN: SORRY EYES

16

HOMECOMING

"All journeys eventually end in the same place, home."

-Chris Geiger

11-25-04
Thanksgiving Day in the U.S

TRAVEL BROCHURE DESCRIPTION:

**Day 19: KATHMANDU • 4,383 feet and Day 20: Home –
200 feet above sea level**

No trekking company menus anymore. Time to celebrate.

Late evening

Today is the first Thanksgiving of my life that I am not celebrating with my family. Before booking this trip many months ago, the thought of missing Thanksgiving in order to go on this trek gave me second thoughts. I wasn't sure what to do, but I ultimately decided to move forward with it based on a number of other factors. Now, thinking back over the past couple of weeks, I'm wondering if God punished me for leaving my family. Maybe this was my "sentence" for not being at home with them. Or, just maybe, it was God's way of telling me to never attempt to summit Mount Everest in the future. Whatever the case, I heard the message loud and clear.

Although I was missing Thanksgiving dinner with my family, I managed to have a delicious breakfast buffet at the hotel today. Food never tasted so good. I know I wouldn't have felt the same way about this buffet a few weeks ago, but after having not eaten for most of the past two weeks, it was a feast.

As I've aged, I have attempted to appreciate whatever I have received, but to be truly grateful for breakfast is something new for me. I have been blessed by having been raised in a middle class family, and having been given most of the basic necessities life in America has to offer. My parents were wonderful and worked hard to raise my siblings and me, providing us with many of the luxuries middle class American kids typically have the good fortune to receive. When I get home, I need to thank them for all they've done. I also need to thank Faith for allowing me to come here without any complaints or stipulations, to pursue my dream – even though it turned out to be a nightmare. I'm a very lucky guy and I need to keep this in mind every single day from here on in.

I said goodbye to everyone on the team. I thanked Lorraine for everything, and also reiterated to her that the decision to take the path less travelled a few days ago was a good one for me, and that I appreciated it no matter what the others had indicated. I wished her the best of luck with starting her business and offered my assistance if she needed it.

I arrived at the Tribhuvan International Airport with two hours to spare. The airport had a tiny, but comfortable, Thai Airways lounge. It immediately reminded me of "home" and all of the many comforts of modern life. As basic as it was, it seemed like a country club.

The flight to Bangkok was uneventful, except for the fact that the rather large foreigner sitting next to me stank. He probably hadn't showered in a month. I had to inhale in the opposite direction from him and then exhale out towards him in order to blow the stench away. I did this for most of the flight so I wouldn't end up gagging. I was almost wishing I were back in the outhouse in Dingboche. Unfortunately, the flight was full, so I couldn't move to another seat. Besides, I was slightly more understanding (after having been on the trek) that he possibly smelled due to the fact that he didn't have the resources to shower as frequently as he may have wanted.

I am now hanging out at another Thai Airways lounge in Bangkok. There are some great food choices and plenty of drink choices besides Fanta Orange. I had a Thai dinner a couple of hours ago, which included my favorites, pad Thai and green curry chicken. The curry sauce was fiery hot, causing my body temperature to rise a few degrees. I mixed it with some rice, and for the first time in two weeks my taste buds came alive.

I'm going to attempt to stay awake tonight at the airport and force myself into the time zone back home. I have a few hours until my next flight early tomorrow morning. I figure this will help prevent significant jet lag next week when I'm back at work.

Speaking of work, I haven't taken three weeks of vacation – if that's what you could call the past few weeks – in fourteen years. I certainly didn't enjoy myself as I would have on a beach vacation, but I definitely didn't think of work for one moment. I was way too focused on many other more important issues than to worry about the (relatively) minor business issues I would typically be concerned about at the office.

THE TREK

This will be my final journal entry. I'm now on the last leg of my trip back home to New York from Tokyo. I ate enough dumplings at the airport to hold me over for at least a week.

Now that it's all coming to an end, I can try to answer the obvious question, the same question dozens of friends and family members will be asking me when I arrive back home. Did I enjoy the trek? Short answer, no. I was miserable during most of this trek except for the last two days. I derived little joy from it.

So maybe I should rephrase the question, by asking "Was it worth it?" Well, from a purely economic perspective, I can, again, easily say no. I was an absolute idiot to pay as much as I did for this punishment. I could have found plenty of people to torture me for much less money and without having to travel half-way around the world.

Beyond pure dollars, however, I honestly do need to give the question more serious consideration. So, let's start with the easiest question first. What went wrong? Well, almost everything – but I've already given you all of the gory details as to why. So I'll just touch on just one overriding point. It simply never occurred to me how dire things could get – being so very ill while living in the crippling cold, consistently, for days on end – with no way out. Combined with the high altitude symptoms, the arduous physical demands, the harsh environmental conditions, and the lack of both sleep and nutrition, it became a recipe for disaster and resulted in utter despair.

Incredibly, as difficult as it is for me to believe, I now have other health issues – basically aftereffects from the past couple of weeks of trekking. I think my adrenaline enabled me to get through the tail end of the trek, suppressing my afflictions for a couple of days and leading me to incorrectly believe that my health was improving. However, at this moment, my lips are bleeding – in multiple places along my aging lip lines. They are severely chapped from the cold, dry weather, and the bright sun which reflected off the snow. They are as coarse as sandpaper. My nose, which ran like a leaky faucet the entire trip, is terribly raw and painfully sensitive to the slightest touch. I went through two boxes of tissues the first couple of days of the trek, and then resorted to using whatever else I could find to wipe it, which typically was cardboard-like toilet paper. And, as long as I'm on the subject of toilet paper and soreness, my butt crack has almost been chafed to the bone. The hundred or so visits to the outhouse, in conjunction with the dysentery and the low quality toilet paper, have resulted in the worst case of diaper rash in the history of mankind.

All I can say is that I owe a huge "thank you" to the person who invented Cipro. If not for him or her, as well as Jay, my drug supplier, I probably would have been air-evacuated off the mountain in Dingboche over a week ago. [A few days after returning home, I discovered I had a virus (and ulcers) in my throat from taking too much Cipro. It had not only killed off the bad bacteria causing the dysentery, it also killed off much of the good bacteria in my body. I took a terrible risk staying on it for as long as I did. My family thought it was crazy that I wasn't talking their ears off by telling them all about the trek, but it hurt too much to speak. Fortunately, they had my journal, which Faith read to all of the girls.]

So basically, this was one entirely "sick" adventure. Yet, as hard as it may be to believe, there was some good that came out of it. First, the scenery was truly mind-blowing and beautiful. It was wondrous seeing Mount Everest, her siblings, and much of the Himalayas for as far as the eye could see. I can say with near-certainty that I'll never be in as glorious a setting again.

Also, as physically difficult as this entire trek was for me, I felt a huge sense of accomplishment after reaching the summit of Kala Patthar. It was through sheer will that I didn't give up. I have never been pushed to the brink of exhaustion as I was pushed on this trek. And now, thinking back to what I had to deal with each day, I'm amazed and proud that I had the fortitude to persevere. Of course, I would have been much happier if I also made it to Base Camp, but it simply wasn't in the cards for me. I am disappointed I didn't get to see it, but just the same, I am satisfied that I had the wisdom - and the courage, as strange as that may seem - to not go. Whatever the case, I'll most certainly never put my body through anything as difficult as this in my lifetime.

Last, I would be remiss if I didn't mention the true heroes of this journey, the Nepalese staff. It was an eye-opening experience seeing the Sherpas and porters in action. The Sherpas kept us out of harm's way. They watched our backs, mine in particular, as we trekked each day. Our safety was their top priority. And the porters did punishing work from early in the morning until late at night. Through all sorts of treacherous weather, adversity, and even sickness, they didn't blink an eye when asked for something or when doing their job. They are kind and dedicated employees, and giving individuals. They never hesitated with any task. It was always "service with a smile."

After living through this trek, there's no doubt in my mind that the Sherpas and porters of Nepal are the true, under-recognized heroes of almost every Himalayan expedition. In the future, every time I read about another person who has reached the summit of Everest or any other challenging mountain in the Himalayas, I'll know there were a significant number of Sherpas and porters behind the scenes doing much, if not most, of the heavy lifting to ensure the safety and success of the climber.

So was it worthwhile? I guess I have to say yes. I fulfilled a life-long dream. Although it obviously didn't turn out as planned, and it certainly wasn't fun – by any stretch of the imagination – it undoubtedly was, for me, the most significant adventure ever. Adventures aren't necessarily meant to be fun, particularly those at 18,000 feet in third world countries. It was surely memorable, but not at all in the way that I originally anticipated. It was a tremendous experience in which I discovered much about myself, my capabilities, my limitations, human nature – and about a people, place and culture I will never forget.

I am not returning home as a different, or changed, person. This trek was for me, more than anything, a reminder of the things I am always supposed to know, appreciate, and do. It was a reinforcement of many of life's lessons; be thankful for what you have; give your best effort at whatever you do; maintain your health, if at all possible; and above all, cherish your family, since there is nothing more important. These are obvious things, but generally overlooked or taken for granted by most people. If I can remember these very basic things, and truly practice them for the rest of my life, then the last two weeks of misery wasn't such a terrible price to pay.

My goal when I get home is to spend less time at work so I can spend more time with my family, as well as take better care of my body. The next journey I take will be with my family, and will be some place warm.

* **

When I cleared U.S. Customs and saw my family at the airline terminal waiting for me with a big sign reading, "WELCOME HOME," I was overjoyed. Seeing the three smiling faces on my little girls brought instant warmth to my heart. They were stunned to see only 88% of their dad, since I had lost the balance of my body weight (twenty pounds) in only three weeks. They were also surprised that all I had with me when I arrived were the clothes on my body, my favorite backpack containing my sleeping bag, and a few souvenirs for them. They had seen an entire room full of hiking gear prior to my departure to Nepal. It was all gone. I had given it away to the Sherpas and porters, including the duffel bag. Of course, I discarded the bag of underwear marked "BIOHAZARD" when I arrived at the hotel in Kathmandu.

Since I was barely able to speak because of my virus, I gave my girls huge hugs and squeezed them as tightly as I could and whispered, "I love you," to them. Faith and I hugged, looked at each other, and we both rolled our eyes and shook our heads side to side, acknowledging the ordeal was over and we could both breathe a sigh of relief. I softly murmured, "Let's go home."

THE END

EPILOGUE

"The only journey is the one within."

- Ranier Maria Rilke

I had yearned to go to the Himalayas for so long. It was a self-fulfilling fascination so deeply embedded in me that I actually believed it would help me find my "holy grail" of happiness or my own personal utopia. It didn't. Quite the opposite: the journey to nirvana unexpectedly turned into a living nightmare.

When people ask me to describe the physical issues I dealt with on the trek, I tell them that if they want to understand what I went through, they should do the following: Pack your bags for two weeks and go to a supermarket and have someone lock you inside the meat locker for two continuous weeks, with no escape. Before you do, make sure you have a bad cold or better yet, the flu. The thermostat should initially be set at the freezing point and it should be lowered each day by a couple of degrees for the first ten days, and lowered a further ten degrees each evening and through the night. Don't bring anything nutritious to eat. As a matter of fact, don't eat much of anything at all (except for a few energy bars), since the smell and sight of the raw meat in the meat locker, over two weeks, should nauseate you enough to make your stomach turn. Optimally, during your two-week frosty stay, you should eat some tainted pork in order to attempt to give yourself food poisoning for a couple of days. And of course, have access to a dirty sink from which to drink contaminated water. You'll also need to have three things delivered to the meat locker in advance of your departure; a stair master machine to climb an

233

average of six hours per day, a case of Fanta orange soda, and, most important, a port-a-potty for going to the bathroom – one already completely full of human waste. Make sure the deliverymen drop it a few times before it is placed inside the meat locker, so the feces spread out everywhere inside of it...in order to get the full effect. And by the way, even if you are actually capable of doing all of this, it wouldn't even scratch the surface of what else you'd experience at the high altitude, but hopefully you get the point.

You never know where and when a journey will end, even after you think you've completed it. The two-week trek was only the first leg of what turned out to be a much longer journey. The second leg was writing this book. It was a test of my willingness to dig into my past and recall events, some good and some bad, some funny and some sad, which I had stored away deep in the file cabinets of my brain. I had long forgotten about so many of these childhood experiences. Reliving them was enlightening. It helped me to understand what it was that had caused me to fall in love with nature, why I was so driven to succeed, and why I had always pushed myself to take on challenges that most other individuals have no desire to pursue.

I mentioned at the start of this book that prior to the trek I had thought my life was lacking. I ultimately realized it was, more than anything else, the emptiness of working too hard at my job and sacrificing quality time with my family in the process. When I returned home, I immediately cut back my hours to a more moderate workday. I spent the extra time having dinner with my family, playing with my kids, going to their school and sporting events, getting in shape and generally taking time to "admire the view from the top of the mountain."

If it weren't for the trek, it's very possible that I'd still be working way too many hours, travelling for business constantly, and I'd be completely out of shape. And, I would have missed out on some of the greatest moments of my kids' lives.

A few years ago, I decided to take on another challenge – to climb Mt. Kilimanjaro in Tanzania. It was only a five-day trek, even though it's approximately 1,000 feet higher than Kala Patthar. It was a mountain more to my liking – a straight-up climb – versus the "ups and downs" in the Himalayas. I successfully reached the summit of the highest point in Africa, at 19,341 feet, with a few friends by my side.

Although I promised myself after coming home from Nepal I would never climb another high altitude mountain again, just four years later I had forgotten the emotional roller coaster and physical pain I endured previously...or maybe I sub-consciously decided to block out the bad memories. Either way, I decided once again to challenge myself (I had also put on a few pounds and needed to lose some weight.) I of course had dysentery, developed altitude sickness and was miserably cold. And yes, the outhouses were as disgusting as in the Himalayas. Luckily, however, I had a much better understanding of what was in store for me prior to arriving. (Once again, when I arrived home, I promised myself and my family that I would never go on another high altitude trek. So far, I've kept this promise.)

I still love trekking, but generally in the spring, summer and fall – I can't handle the extreme cold anymore. There's no better way for me to get in shape and stay healthy – and being surrounded by nature enables me to eliminate any stress. My family brings me joy, but nature provides me with a level of serenity I can't seem to find any other way. Best of all, my family now comes along with me on many of my hikes. Although they admittedly don't love hiking, they do it because they know I do. And yet, when they reach the summit, they feel a tremendous sense of joy and accomplishment. And their joy is my nirvana.

EPILOGUE

About the author

D avid Schachne fell in love with the great outdoors at an early age, while growing up in Brooklyn. An avid hiker and fitness enthusiast, he began writing in his mid-twenties, while earning his Masters degree at Harvard Business School. He always had a strong desire to write - about anything - but instead focused on his business career for over twenty years, spending most of his time writing business proposals instead of manuscripts. After 9/11, he decided to pursue his passion and started writing more extensively, combining it with his passion for hiking. He has hiked in many places around the world and has reached the summits of some of the tallest mountains in the U.S. and elsewhere. He has served on the boards of two successful businesses, as well as Make-a-Wish of CT. He resides in Connecticut with his wife and three daughters.

Made in the USA
San Bernardino, CA
28 September 2013